TAKE THE LAW INTO YOUR OWN HANDS™

Debtors'
Rights

A Legal Self-Help Guide

With Forms

Second Edition

By Gudrun M. Nickel
Attorney at Law

SPHINX PUBLISHING
Sphinx International, Inc.
1725 Clearwater-Largo Rd. S.
Post Office Box 25
Clearwater, FL 34617
Tel: (813) 587-0999

SPHINX®
is a registered trademark of Sphinx International, Inc.

Note: The law changes constantly and is subject to different interpretations. It is up to you
to check it thoroughly before relying on it.
Neither the author nor the publisher guarantees the outcome of the uses to which this
material is put.

Table of Contents

Introduction 7

Using Self-Help Law Books 11

Chapter 1. Types of Debt — An Overview 13
Secured Debt 13
How Unsecured Debt May Become Secured Debt 13
Selling Your Secured Property 14
When the Lender Sells the Collateral 14
The Bank's Right of Set-Off 14
Unsecured Debt 15
Debt Assumed in Divorce 15
Contingent Liabilities 16
Business Debt 16
Student Loans 18
Child Support 20

Chapter 2. Strategies Before Creditors and Collectors Call 23
Prepare Yourself and Your Creditors.. 23
The Minimum One Dollar Payment Myth 24
Wage Assignments 24
Credit Counseling 24

Chapter 3. When the Collection Agency Calls 25
What is a Collection Agency? 25
What Can a Collection Agency Do? 25
Your First Call From a Collector 26
What a Collection Agency Cannot Do 27
If You Have an Attorney 32
What You Can Do On Your Own 32
For Further Research 33
Sample Letters 34

Chapter 4. Consumer Reporting Agencies and Your Credit Report 37
What is a Consumer Reporting Agency?...................................... 37
Information a Consumer Reporting Agency May Furnish 37
Obtaining Information From the Agency's Files 38
Items Your Report Cannot Contain 39
What to Do if You Dispute Information in Your Report 39
Cost of the Report.. 41
Reports for Employment Purposes 41
Requirements for Users of Reports... 41
Use of Other Information 42
Obtaining Information Under False Pretenses 42
Providing Information to an Unauthorized Person. 42
Liability of Reporting Agency for Non-Compliance. 42
For Further Research 43
Sample letters 44

Chapter 5. The Internal Revenue Service 49
    Collection of Money Owed to the IRS 49
    Don't Assume an IRS Bill is Correct 49
    Don't Leave an IRS Inquiry Unanswered 50
    Property the IRS Can Take for Taxes Due 50
    Taxpayers Bill of Rights 50
    What the IRS Cannot Take 50
    IRS Time Limitations 51
    If Your Tax Return is Audited 51
    What You Can Do. 52
    For Further Research 53
    Sample IRS Correspondence 54
    Small Tax Case Petition Form 55

Chapter 6. Loan Disclosure Requirements — Truth in Lending 57
    The Federal Law 57
    Required Disclosures 58
    Time Periods in Which Disclosures Must be Made. 59
    Finance Charge and Annual Percentage Rate (APR) 60
    Good Faith Estimate — Residential Mortgages. 62
    Equity Line Mortgages and Your Right to Rescind 62
    Balloon Payments on Consumer Loans 64
    Refinancing 64
    When Disclosure is Not Required 64
    Lenders' Liabilities and Your Rights and Obligations. 65
    For Further Research. 66
    Truth in Lending Disclosure 66
    Sample Disclosure Form 67
    Sample Good Faith Estimate 68
    Sample Compliance Agreement 69
    Sample Notice of Right to Cancel. 70

Chapter 7. Credit Cards & Other Open End Consumer Credit Loans 71
    What is Open-End Credit? 71
    Information That Must be Disclosed 71
    Billing Disclosure Requirements 72
    Penalties for Violations. 73
    Consumer Loan Billing Procedures 73
    Unsolicited Credit Cards 74
    When a Credit Card is Lost or Stolen 74
    For Further Research. 75
    Sample Letter 76

Chapter 8. Consumer Lease Disclosures 77
    What is a Consumer Lease?. 77
    Disclosure Requirements 77
    Residual Value Calculation 79
    Penalties or Other Charges 79
    Liabilities of Lessor for Violations 79
    For Further Research. 80

Chapter 9. Real Estate Loan Foreclosure 81

Mortgages 81

Contract or Agreement for Deed 82

Deed of Trust 82

Read Your Loan Documents 83

The Mortgage Foreclosure Process. 83

Service of Process and Deficiency Judgments 83

After the sale — Period of Redemption 84

Foreclosing a Deed of Trust 85

What if You Sell the Property Before Foreclosure? 85

Deed in Lieu of Foreclosure 86

Negotiating With Your Lender and FHA Extensions 87

If You Are in the Military 88

Recap — Steps You Can Take After Foreclosure is Started 88

For Further Research 90

Responding to a Foreclosure Complaint 91

Sample Answer to Foreclosure Complaint 92

Chapter 10. Repossession of Personal Property — Foreclosure 95

Restrictions on Repossession 96

Sale of Collateral After Repossession 96

Lender's Pattern of Accepting Late Payments 97

Your Remedies 98

If the Lender Already Has the Collateral 99

For Further Research 99

Chapter 11. When the Creditor Files a Lawsuit 101

What is a Judgment? 101

How a Creditor Gets a Judgment 101

Your Defenses to the Petition or Complaint 103

What if You Move to Another State? 104

Confession of Judgment 105

Possible Alternatives if the Debt is Legitimate. 105

Effect of Judgment on Credit Report 106

For Further Research 106

Sample Answer to Complaint 107

Sample Motion 108

Chapter 12. Collection of Money Judgments 109

Actions by a Judgment Creditor 109

When the Creditor Knows What Assets You Have 111

Garnishments 111

Writ of Execution and Levy 114

Attachment of Property Not Yet in Your Possession 115

Attachment of Property Before Judgment 115

For Further Research 116

Chapter 13. Bankruptcy as an Option 117

What is Bankruptcy? 117

Types of Bankruptcy 118

How Bankruptcy Works 118
Bankruptcy Will Not Eliminate All of Your Debts 119
The Bankruptcy Court Will Not Take All of Your Property 119
What are the Pros and Cons? 121
How to File for Bankruptcy 122
For Further Research 122

Chapter 14. Property Exempt from Creditors 123
State by State Homestead Exemptions 125
State by State Garnishment Exemptions 130

Chapter 15. Personal Assessment and Planning for the Future 137
Debt and Asset Evaluation 137
Making Yourself "Judgment Proof" 138
Personal Financial Assessment Form 139

Glossary 143

Appendix A.   U.S. Government Printing Offices 147

Appendix B.   State by State Consumer Affairs Offices 149

Appendix C.   Federal Trade Commission Regional Offices 153

Appendix D.   Statutes of Limitations 154

Appendix E.   Frequently Referenced Laws 156

Index 157

Acknowledgment

To my husband, Bob, for his invaluable contribution.

Introduction

As each week brings news of corporate downsizing and jobs being replaced by automation, more Americans are finding themselves out of work for the first time. The period of unemployment for those laid off is becoming longer and many people will never find a job at the same salary they had gotten used to.

Even the most responsible and conscientious person can experience a change in economic circumstances which may be financially and psychologically devastating. Lifetime careers sometimes die an early death; if you become ill, there's often too little or no disability insurance. A job loss or illness can make it difficult, if not impossible, to meet your financial obligations. Lenders who were once pursuing you to lend you money will soon pursue you to get the money back if you fail to make the required payments. The only way to avoid having creditors is to avoid having any debt. However, most people have a mortgage on their homes, have purchased one or several vehicles on credit, may have a consumer loan for household items, and have a number of credit cards. Your creditors—mortgage and finance companies, banks, credit card companies, etc.—all expect to get paid.

When you don't pay, your creditor has a number of options available in attempting to collect an outstanding debt. The creditor can:

- Send your account to a collection agency. The agency rather than the creditor will then write and call you to try to collect the payment. (If the creditor assigns its right to the account, the collection agency can sue for the amount due in its own name.)

- Report your unpaid bill directly to a credit reporting service (credit bureau), and then send it to a collection agency.
- Get a judgment against you in court.
- Foreclose on your real estate and get a deficiency judgment if the sale proceeds aren't enough to cover the debt.
- Repossess your personal property which is used as security for a loan, sell it, and get a deficiency judgment if the amount of the sale isn't enough to cover the debt.
- Get an assignment of property you are expecting to receive, such as a tax return or royalties.
- Take your property, either before or after getting a judgment against you.
- Garnish your wages.
- Force you into bankruptcy.

Although most people don't openly discuss financial problems, they are a reality of life, particularly in an economy where thousands of people are being laid-off or terminated from their jobs. Even if you're getting unemployment benefits, they may not be sufficient to meet the financial obligations you took on while earning a good wage or salary. It is easy to become overwhelmed by the pressure of collectors' calls and a mailbox full of overdue bills. Being served with a summons in a lawsuit filed by a creditor to collect an unpaid debt—a good possibility if your bills are overdue—is an experience most people would rather live without.

Becoming overwhelmed or having anxiety attacks doesn't solve financial problems. In order to deal with financial setbacks effectively, it is important to have an understanding of what your rights are, the extent to which a creditor can actually go in collecting a debt, and how you can defend yourself against the actions your creditors might take to collect those debts.

This book will explain what types of actions creditors can take against you for non-payment and what your possible defenses to those actions are. This book also contains information about your rights under Federal law regarding collection agencies, credit reporting, consumer loans, credit cards, and leases. The Federal laws apply if you enter into a written agreement with the creditor regarding the debt; *and* the extension of credit is for personal, family, or household purposes; *and* if the creditor (or collector) involved, during the immediately preceding calendar year, entered into agreements with consumers involving interest or finance charges, *or* extensions of credit involving more than four installments more than twenty five times; *and* payments are to be made in more than four installments *or* interest is added which wasn't previously charged. An isolated transaction with someone to whom you owe money will probably not be regulated by Federal law;

however, there may be state laws for your protection. (The chapters dealing with judgments and collections will still apply, whether or not your loan or lease transaction is subject to Federal law.)

In a good economy, lenders readily give credit to most people—many lenders even have employees whose sole job is to find borrowers to whom they would like to make a loan. In some cases, perhaps lenders were overly zealous in their efforts to extend credit to you, and now, when times are tough, you may find it difficult to repay those obligations. There are numerous laws which have been enacted to protect borrowers from certain lender and creditor tactics, and you may find that you indeed have some recourse.

Having a better understanding of the different types of debt you have incurred, and what your legal rights are in the event of your inability to repay a loan or credit obligation, will help you take control of whatever financial dilemma you may find yourself in. You should take some comfort in knowing that you can no longer be put into prison for simply being in debt. (Two states, Wisconsin and Rhode Island, still allow imprisonment for certain debt, but the debtor must be released after swearing to the judge that he has no money or property with which to pay the debt.) Being in debt should be viewed as a temporary condition—in which you may find yourself due to present circumstances. It is a condition that can be changed, through your own efforts in dealing with creditors or perhaps ultimately filing a bankruptcy petition. The most important point to keep in mind is that all hope is not lost—and with the information available to you in this book, you will also be better able to protect yourself from financial problems in the future.

Some chapters include a section on how to exercise your rights or defenses, with some sample letters and forms. You should use these in conjunction with other resources available to you, including your local law library (often your local library will have books which contain your state as well as Federal laws), your State or district attorney's office, your local court clerk, and your state or local consumer affairs or public service office. The state offices are listed at the back of this book as Appendix B.

There may be a Government Printing Office bookstore in your area which has publications available regarding the federal Truth-in-Lending disclosure requirements, the Fair Credit Billing Act, the Fair Credit Reporting Act, the Fair Credit Leasing Act, and other pertinent information. See Appendix A. For your convenience and for further research, the sources of information are listed at the end of each chapter. Information about credit and your rights as a consumer is available from Consumer Information, Pueblo, Colorado 81009.

You will find that the terms "lender" and "creditor" are used repeatedly. Although there may be a technical difference in that a lender is in the business of lending money, while a creditor is in the business of extending credit (such as a credit card company), the terms are used interchangeably.

Using Self-Help Law Books

Whenever you shop for a product or service you are faced with a variety of different levels of quality and price. In deciding upon which one to buy you make a cost/value analysis based upon your willingness to pay and the quality you desire.

When buying a car you decide whether you want transportation, comfort, status or sex appeal, and you decide among such choices as a Chevette, a Lincoln, a Rolls Royce or a Porsche. Before making a decision you usually weigh the merits of each against the cost.

When you get a headache, you can take a pain reliever such as aspirin or you can go to a medical specialist for a neurological examination. Given this choice most people, of course, take a pain reliever, since it only costs pennies whereas a medical examination would cost hundreds of dollars and take a lot of time. This is usually a very logical choice because very rarely is anything more than a pain reliever needed for a headache. But in some cases a headache may indicate a brain tumor and failing to go to a specialist right away can result in complications. Should everyone with a headache go to a specialist? Of course not, but people treating their own illnesses must realize that they are taking a chance, based upon their cost/value analysis of the situation, that they are taking the most logical option.

The same cost/value analysis must be made in deciding to do one's own legal work. Many legal situations are very simple, requiring a simple form and no complicated analysis. Anyone with a little intelligence and a book of instructions can handle the matter simply.

But there is always the chance that there is a complication involved which only a lawyer would notice. To simplify the law into a book like this, often several legal cases must be condensed into a single sentence or paragraph. Otherwise, the book would be several hundred pages long and too complicated for most people. However, this simplification necessarily leaves out many details and nuances which would apply to special or unusual situations. Also, there are many ways to interpret most legal questions. Your case may come before a judge who disagrees with the analysis of our author.

Therefore, in deciding to use a self-help law book and to do your own legal work you must realize that you are making a cost/value analysis and deciding that the chance that your case will not turn out to your satisfaction is outweighed by the money you will save by doing it yourself. Most people doing their own simple legal matters will probably never have a problem. But occasionally someone may find out that it ended up costing them more to have an attorney straighten out the situation than it would have if they had hired an attorney to begin with. Keep this in mind while handling your case and be sure to consult an attorney if you feel you might need further guidance.

Chapter 1
Types of Debt — an Overview

Secured Debt

All debts are either secured or unsecured. When an interest in property is given to your lender to make the loan safe, you have a "secured" debt. Examples of secured debt are your home mortgage and your car loan. The lender puts everyone on notice about its interest in your property by filing a mortgage on your real estate or a security interest in your personal property in the appropriate county or state records. The lender will secure its interest in a car or mobile home by placing its lien directly on the title. In any case where the lender has taken the proper steps to record its interest, you cannot sell the property without either paying off the lender or having the buyer take the property subject to the lender's interest. The property given as security is also referred to as "collateral."

The lender may also take an interest in personal property by taking possession of it. For example, if you have given the lender stocks and bonds as collateral for your loan, the lender may hold these until the loan is paid off, prohibiting you from using the same stocks and bonds as collateral for other loans or from selling them.

How Unsecured Debt May Become Secured Debt

An unsecured debt may become a secured debt if a judgment becomes a lien on your property. Even without judgments, some states

allow liens to be filed. In Florida, for example, condominium associa-
tions generally have the right, without first getting a judgment, to place
a lien on your property if you do not pay your condominium association
assessments. Likewise, people whom you employ to work on your
property or provide material may be able to file a lien before getting a
judgment if you do not pay them. A judgment may also become a lien
on your property. Ultimately, the lienholder may take the property and
foreclose its lien, just like a creditor to whom you actually gave a
security interest in your property. (See Chapters 9 & 10.)

Selling Your Secured Property

If liens are not paid when you sell your property, they are not
removed even if you transfer title. You may have considered selling to
get out from under a mortgage obligation, however, a sale of property
given as security will not necessarily relieve you of your responsibility
to pay the mortgage holder, unless he agrees to let you off the hook and
let your buyer take over the payments. (See Chapter 9.) If you do not
make the loan payments, the lender may, by proper legal proceedings
and as specifically spelled out in the loan documents, take the property
you have given as collateral. If the other lienholders are not paid when
you sell, they can foreclose against you and the new title holder. (As for
stocks, bonds, and items which the lender can hold in its possession, the
lender can then sell them to pay off the debt.)

When the Lender Sells the Collateral

After the lender sells the collateral, depending upon your loan
agreement, he will then apply the money from the sale, less expenses,
to your loan. This does not necessarily mean that you are no longer
liable to your lender. The loan document you signed may also give the
lender the right to get a "deficiency judgment" against you if the
amount realized from the sale is not enough to pay the balance due on
the loan. Deficiency judgments are also discussed in other chapters in
this book.

The Bank's Right of Set-Off

If you have several accounts at one bank as well as a loan, and you
fail to make your payments on the loan, the lender may have the right
to take the money from your deposit accounts and apply it to your debt.
This is called the bank's "right of set-off."

However, the bank may do this *only* if this was disclosed to you in
the loan documents. The bank cannot use your other accounts as

collateral without meeting the disclosure requirement. Otherwise, you can sue the bank for damages, including any cost to you for overdrawn checks. (See Chapter 6.) If the bank has issued you a credit card, it is prohibited from taking funds from other accounts to pay any outstanding amount on the card. (See Chapter 7.)

Unsecured Debt

An unsecured loan is one for which the lender has taken no collateral. Most credit cards and any loan given to you requiring only your signature are unsecured loans. (The signature of someone guaranteeing payment, or a co-signer, is given as security for the debt.) Unsecured debt also includes any amount you owe for services, such as doctor's bills. The service provider (i.e. hospital, doctor, dentist, accountant) and the creditor of unsecured debt will often first try to contact you personally in an attempt to work out payment of the outstanding bill.

Debt Assumed in Divorce

A property settlement agreement with your ex-spouse does not relieve you of any debt you jointly obligated yourselves to pay. If, for example, you and your ex-spouse used a joint credit card, you will both be held liable for payment. A property settlement agreement may specifically spell out which spouse will take over payment of certain bills. However, if your former spouse fails to make the payments as required under your agreement, the creditor will look to you for the money. You can argue that by agreement he or she is responsible for the debt. Unless the creditor released you from any obligation to pay, you may still be held responsible.

> For example, Bruce had been divorced for over a year and was planning to remarry. Before his remarriage he received notice that his former wife had filed bankruptcy, thereby eliminating her obligation on the debts she had agreed to pay. The property settlement Bruce had reached with her, and which was filed in the court records, described each debt and which party would accept responsibility for payment. However, the creditors had not released Bruce, and when his wife filed for bankruptcy, they looked to Bruce for payment. Bruce was able to manage fine with his portion of the debt as divided in the settlement agreement, but was unable to carry his former spouse's financial obligations as well. Bruce filed for Chapter 7 bankruptcy.

This is also true of your day-to-day service providers. For example, even if your former spouse has agreed to pay your child's medical bills, you may be held responsible. If you take your child for medical treatment, the physician will most likely look to you for payment. The physician is not a party to any agreement you may have with a former spouse. If possible, you should make advance arrangements with your former spouse and the service provider for payment of these types of bills, so that ultimately non-payment won't have a negative effect on your credit report.

Finally, if your former spouse kept the family residence and agreed to make the mortgage payments, you may have given him a "quit claim deed" and assumed that you had no further liability. However, if you have any doubt about his financial reliability, you should consider checking periodically to make sure the payments are current. If the lender forecloses, you will be named in the lawsuit as a defendant, since you are still obligated on the mortgage.

Contingent Liabilities

If you have a "contingent liability," you will be liable for payment to a creditor only in the event the primary borrower does not pay. For example, if you have personally guaranteed payment of a business loan and the business can no longer make the payments, the creditor will look to you for the balance owed. Likewise, if you co-sign on a loan for your daughter to buy a car, and she stops making the payments, the lender will come to you. You may be held responsible and pursued by the creditor as with any other debt.

Business Debt

If you own your business and the business is having financial difficulties, these difficulties may affect your personal financial situation as well.

As a new business, you may have entered into leases for space and other legal contracts. If operating as a sole proprietorship, you will be held personally responsible for any contract or agreement you enter into. Likewise, signing as a partner does not insulate you from personal liability; all partners are usually responsible for partnership debt. You may have set up your business as a corporation, which is considered a separate, legal entity. Although a corporation usually shields its stockholders-owners from liability, you may still have personal liability as an officer or director. For example, while you may have assumed that setting up your new business as a corporation would relieve you of personal responsibility, your creditors and landlords probably required that you sign "personally," or that you personally guarantee the corporation's obligation. In other words, if the corporation goes out of business before it has met its obligation under a particular contract, (for example, if the corporation vacates leased space before the end of the lease term) you may be held personally liable for the remaining obligation.

As a defense against any action against you personally for your corporation's obligation, you will need to show that *only* the corporation signed the contract, and that you signed *as president (or other officer) of the corporation* and not individually. (See Chapter 11.) If you have signed a personal guaranty for any corporate obligation, determine whether it was for a secured debt. In other words, is the creditor able to take the collateral as payment for the balance owed? (Your guaranty may be "conditional," requiring the creditor to first take the collateral, or "unconditional," allowing the creditor to come directly to you for payment regardless of the collateral.) While your guaranty of payment might not require the creditor to first take the collateral in satisfaction of the debt, the creditor may be willing to do so to minimize any potential losses, particularly if the creditor believes that you may personally not be able to pay the amount due. As for business leases which you have personally guaranteed, the landlord may be obligated to minimize its losses by finding another tenant as quickly as possible. (State laws vary on this issue.) However, any landlord attempting to obtain a judgment against you personally for the balance due on a lease may find the court much more receptive if he can show that he made a diligent effort to re-lease the space. You should do your best to help the landlord in finding a new tenant to minimize your liability under the guaranty. Even if the law doesn't require the landlord to attempt to minimize its damages, your efforts may discourage the landlord from proceeding against you for the full amount due on the lease.

If there is any question as to whether the guaranty is legally valid and enforceable by the landlord, you should discuss this with an attorney.

If you have signed a document for payment of an obligation containing the words "joint and several liability," along with other owners of your business, don't assume that you will be responsible for repayment only to the extent of your share in the business. "Joint and several liability" means that each of those individuals who signed the document are individually as well as jointly liable for the total amount due. You may be liable for the entire amount due if the other guarantors do not pay. Creditors usually pursue the signor with the greatest ability to repay the debt. If the creditor pursues you, make him aware of your personal financial situation. You may be able to reach an agreement with the creditor for payment, then pursue the other guarantors for indemnification.

Aside from the corporate obligations you may have personally guaranteed, you must keep in mind that, as an officer of the corporation, owner of the business or partner in a partnership, you have other responsibilities and liabilities. The most important of these are payroll taxes. As the business owner or authorized signer on the account from which payroll taxes are paid, you are personally obligated for the amount which the business deducted from the employees' wages and failed to send to the IRS. In other words, if your bookkeeper fails to make the deposits when due, or if the business ceases operation and taxes are still owed, you may be held personally liable for payment. If this is in fact the case, you should consider the same suggestions for dealing with the Internal Revenue Service as are set forth in Chapter 5.

Student Loans

If you had financial help with your college expenses through a student loan, chances are that repayment was guaranteed by the federal government. In other words, if the loan was made to you by a bank and you failed to pay, the bank looked to the federal government for the money.

Following either your graduation or withdrawal from school, you had a grace period (typically six months) before beginning to repay the loan. The bank, school or other lender could collect the loan itself, or could sell the loan to the Student Loan Marketing Association (SLMA, or "Sallie Mae") for collection. The SLMA is a corporation set up by the Federal government for the sole purpose of collecting outstanding student loan obligations. The U.S. Department of Education may attempt to collect the balance due if SLMA is unsuccessful.

Both SLMA and the Federal Department of Education will report your delinquent student loans to the credit reporting agencies (credit bureaus), and may take other action such as to sue for collection or intercept your income tax refunds.

If you are in default on a federally guaranteed loan, but are now able to start making payments, you may be able to bring the loan out of default by making a certain number of regular, consecutive monthly payments. Contact the guaranty agency that has your loan to find out what you need to do to bring the loan out of default.

If you borrowed money from your college or university and the loan was not Federally guaranteed, the same options are open to the institution as to any other creditor, such as reporting your delinquent account to a credit reporting agency, hiring a collection agency, and filing a lawsuit. The school may also refuse to give you your transcript and your diploma, as well as refuse to allow you to re-enroll. On the other hand, you have the same options as with any other creditor, including negotiating a smaller payment amount.

Your Options

Your options will depend upon the type of student loan. There are basically six types of federally guaranteed student loans:

1. Stafford Loans (formerly called Guaranteed Student Loans).
2. Perkins Loans (formerly called National Direct Student Loans).
3. Federal Supplemental Loans for Students.
4. Health Professions Student Loans.
5. Health Education Assistance Loans.
6. Federal Parental Loans for Students.

Each of these programs has its own unique rules regarding repayment and collection.

Depending upon the type of loan you have, you may have one or more of the following options if you are unable to pay:

•Cancellation of the loan.
•Deferment of payments.
•Negotiating for temporary suspension or reduction of payments.
•Consolidating your loans.
•Filing for bankruptcy.

We will now consider each of these separately.

Cancellation. Again depending upon the type of loan you have, full or partial cancellation is generally available if you die or become disabled; serve in the U.S. military; are employed full-time as a nurse, medical technician, or law enforcement or corrections officer; are a Peace Corps or VISTA volunteer; are a Head Start program staff member; are a teacher in certain low-income areas, of handicapped children, or of math, science, foreign languages or in other designated "teacher-shortage" areas; or return to school to work for a teaching certificate. For more information, call the holder of your loan or the U.S. Department of Education at 1-800-621-3115.

Cancellation of the debt may also be possible in certain cases of fraud or misrepresentation by a trade school. In the past, there were numerous trade schools (for such occupations as truck driving, cosmetology, computer operation and repair, etc.) that got students to take out a government loan and turn the money over to the school, then closed the school before the course was completed. Other schools failed to provide sufficient education to allow the student to obtain employment once the course was completed. If your trade school closed before you could complete the course of study, you were falsely certified to be eligible for the program, or you were entitled to a refund you never got, you may be able to have your loan cancelled. For more information contact the Department of Education and ask for a list of closed schools, or contact your state's Attorney General's office.

Deferment. Typical situations in which deferment may be allowed are where you are enrolled in school, unemployed, on active duty with the military or NOAA , a full-time teacher in a teacher-shortage area, disabled, completing an internship program, on parental leave, the mother of preschool children, or suffering economic hardship. Depending upon the type of loan, the deferment may be of both principle and interest, or of just principle (meaning you will have to make interest-only payment for the deferment period). For more information, contact your loan holder. Ask for a deferment application.

Negotiation As with any other loan, you can always contact the holder of the loan, explain your situation, and try to arrange for payments to be temporarily suspended or reduced. If you don't have any luck negotiating an arrangement you can live with, contact your local Consumer Credit Counseling Service. Maybe they will be able to negotiate a better deal.

Consolidation. If you have more than one student loan, you may be able to consolidate them at a lower interest rate, with a lower single payment, and possibly qualify for a deferment. Much will depend upon the types of loans you have, and whether you are in default. For more information contact the holder of your loan, or Sallie Mae at 1-800-524-9100.

Bankruptcy. You will generally hear it said that student loans cannot be discharged in bankruptcy. However, there are a couple of exceptions to this rule, and even if you can't get a discharge you may be able to get some indirect help. It may be possible to have a student loan discharged in bankruptcy if the payments first became due more than seven years before filing for bankruptcy, or if you can convince the judge that repayment of the loan would cause you undue hardship. If you file for a repayment plan under Chapter 13 of the Bankruptcy Code, and include your student loan in your repayment plan, it will at least stop lawsuits and other harassment over the delinquent loan. Also, if your school is withholding your transcript because of your non-payment, it will have to release the transcript once you notify it of the bankruptcy proceeding, regardless of whether the debt is discharged.

Child Support

A child support obligation is not to be taken lightly. Congress has taken a special interest in payment of child support, and addressed the problem of non-payment by passing the Federal Family Support Act of

1988 and the Revised Uniform Reciprocal Enforcement of Support Act ("URESA"). Under URESA, the District Attorney in your state will be contacted by the District Attorney in your spouse's state regarding the child support due. The District Attorney in your state will then pursue you for the amount.

The law requires your employer to honor a court order to withhold the support payment from your wages. (You can also agree with the other parent or guardian of the child to pay directly.) Remember that you can also be ordered to go to jail for contempt of court if you fail to pay child support, and in some states you may be charged with a misdemeanor.

If you simply cannot pay the amount ordered by the court, you should file a request for modification, explaining the circumstances and why you believe the amount should be reduced. In all states you will generally need to show that your income has decreased so that you are no longer able to pay the amount originally ordered. A sample "Request for Modification" is found at the end of Chapter 11, with examples of reasons for the request. This sample forms shows you how simple it can be to ask for a decrease in child support. You should also obtain a copy of your state's support guidelines. Depending upon your state, the guidelines will be in either the statutes, court rules, or a document from some state agency. If you cannot find them in the statutes or court rules, request a copy from the court clerk or child support enforcement agency. You may find that you are paying more than the guidelines require. If so, you can request a modification.

If your spouse gets a judgment against you for past-due child support, that judgment may also be collected like any other judgment and the same time periods for collection may apply. (See Chapter 12.)

In addition, your income tax refunds may be intercepted and applied to your past due child support. If this occurs, you will receive a notice of the impending tax intercept. The notice will advise you of your right to request some kind of hearing to challenge the taking of your tax refund, and how to go about getting a hearing. Generally, you will only be able to stop the intercept if you have already paid what is owed, or are making regular payments pursuant to an agreement you made for payment of the past due amount (of course, other unusual circumstances may also avoid an intercept, but these are so varied and unusual that they cannot be covered here). If you are remarried and some of the tax refund is for the income of your current spouse, you can apply to the IRS for your spouse's share of the refund. Contact the IRS to obtain the proper form for this.

Chapter 2
Strategies Before Creditors and Collectors Call

Prepare Yourself and Your Creditors

As soon as you realize that you may have difficulties in making your payments, you should contact your creditors. Don't try to hide your financial condition; let them know what has happened—job lay-off, divorce, illness, etc.—and that you will make every effort to meet your financial obligations. Offer to make minimal payments for a period of time, or perhaps suspend your payments (not make any) for a month or more. Generally, your creditors will be much more receptive to your suggestions for reduced or suspended payments if you notify them before they find it necessary to contact you. (Many will accept token payments instead of pursuing collection as long as you explain the reasons for your inability to pay, and that you will make up the difference as soon as you are able.)

You should also take stock of your current financial situation and place your debts and assets in order of priority. (See Chapter 15.) Your most important obligations may be your mortgage or rent, utilities, and car payment. Consider what you can sell in order to pay off some of your debt. Practical strategies, although perhaps a bit difficult to accept at first, will help see you through the tough times. Perhaps you should sell your car, pay off the loan and buy an older, used car which would also lower your insurance premium. However, before selling any property to pay your debt, be sure you understand what will be exempt from judgment creditors and bankruptcy in your state. (See Chapter 14.)

The Minimum One Dollar Payment Myth

Some people have the mistaken notion that a payment of one dollar per month is sufficient, particularly when it comes to hospital and doctor bills, and that no action can be taken by the creditor if that one dollar payment is made regularly. This is an incorrect assumption. Those creditors have the right to receive payment from you in the manner in which you agreed to pay, or in a timely manner.

If you cannot reach an agreement with your creditor as to how a past-due account can be paid, or if you reach an agreement and then do not pay, the creditor can send the past-due account to a collection agency, and ultimately (or in some cases directly) to the credit bureau. The creditor may also choose to pursue a judgment against you, often in a small claims where cases can be handled without a lawyer. However, if your creditor refuses to work with you during your period of financial difficulties, you may have a more sympathetic judge when you are called on to appear in court.

Wage Assignments

Be wary if a creditor asks you to assign some of your wages to make the payments on the loan. This is illegal under Federal law, and it effectively reduces your control over your income. Wage assignments in non-real estate transactions are allowed only if you are also given the power to revoke the assignment. (Title 15 United States Code.)

Credit Counseling

Consumer Credit Counseling. Consumer credit counseling is available through local offices affiliated with the National Foundation for Consumer Credit. Consumer Credit Counseling Services are found in over 400 communities nationwide. This is a non-profit organization, supported by contributions from banks, consumer finance companies, merchants, credit unions, etc. A Consumer Credit Counseling Service can work with your creditors to establish a realistic payment program.

HUD Counseling. There are HUD (Housing Urban Development) approved counseling agencies all over the country. If you are unable to make payments under an FHA mortgage, you will be referred to such an agency. However, counseling assistance is available to anyone, usually at no charge. The counselors can help you get employment, budget your income, and work out your credit difficulties. Contact your local HUD office for information or call the HUD mortgage assistance office in Washington, D.C.

Chapter 3
When the Collection Agency Calls

What is a Collection Agency?

A collection agency is a business whose purpose it is to collect outstanding bills for others. It works as follows: After sending past-due notices and perhaps telephoning, a creditor is unable to collect an outstanding bill from you. The creditor will either contract with a collection agency to collect the bill for the creditor, giving the agency a commission of the amount collected (usually 50 per cent), with the remaining amount then paid to your creditor; or the creditor may sell your account to the collection agency at a discount. When the account has been sold to the agency, the agency can sue on its own behalf to collect the amount due. Child support payments are not "debts" covered by the Fair Debt Collection Practices Act.

What Can a Collection Agency Do?

Beyond sending letters and calling, there is little a collection agency can actually do to collect a debt. In fact, an agency collector once said that, if people knew their legal rights, collection agencies might find it difficult to stay in business. However, you should be aware that if a collection agency is a member of a credit reporting service, your unpaid debt may be reported and will be reflected on your credit report for a period of seven years. (This will be explained in more detail in the next chapter.) Since the collection agency gets paid only on the amounts collected, the collector may use various (and possibly illegal) tactics to get payment from you. Collection agency practices are regulated by the Fair Debt Collection Practices Act.

The Fair Debt Collection Practices Act is a Federal law also known as P.L. 95-109. Congress passed this law to regulate collection agencies and help eliminate abusive debt collection practices which contributed to loss of jobs and invasion of privacy. If a collection agency violates any of the provisions of the law in attempting to collect a debt from you, you may have civil remedies available to you, including punitive damages. (In order for the Act to apply, the debt must have been incurred for personal, family or household purposes.) The Federal Trade Commission is the Federal agency responsible for regulating collection agencies. Under this law, an attorney or law firm can be considered a "collection agency" if regularly engaged in the collection of debts allegedly owed by consumers.

Your First Call From a Collector

Before or no later than five days after your first call from the collection agency, the collector must send you a written notice containing:
- the amount of the debt you supposedly owe;
- the name of the creditor to whom the debt is owed;
- a statement that, unless you dispute the validity of the debt within thirty days, the debt will be assumed to be valid; and a statement that, if you notify the collector in writing within the thirty-day period that the debt, or any portion thereof, is disputed, the collector will get verification and mail it to you;
- a statement that, upon your written request within the thirty-day period, the collector will provide you with the name of the original creditor if different from the current creditor.

Any communication you receive from the collector must clearly state that the purpose of the communication is to collect a debt, and that any information obtained will be used for that purpose.

You have thirty days after receipt of the notice from the collection agency to send written notice back to the agency stating that you do not agree with all or part of the bill, and why, in your opinion, you do not owe the money. (Any subsequent communication by the collector regarding the debt must also include the fact that you have disputed the debt.) The collection agency must then stop all attempts to collect the debt from you until the debt is verified by the creditor and a copy of the verification is sent to you. You may demand that the collector notify any person who received notice of the debt from him within the previous ninety-day period, that the debt has been disputed.

If you do not dispute the debt in writing within the thirty-day period, the collection agency can assume you agree that the amount stated in the notice is accurate, and can continue its collection efforts.

When you receive a call or letter from a collection agency attempting to collect a debt you owed to someone else, there are a number of things you can do. Most importantly, you can simply write a letter and ask that you not be contacted anymore. This, by law, should be enough. However, some collectors use very aggressive and sometimes abusive tactics in order to get payments.

What a Collection Agency Cannot Do

The following is a list of collection agency practices which are among those prohibited under the Fair Debt Collection Practices Act, with suggestions as to what you can do if you believe an agency has violated a provision of the Act.

Remember that these apply to collection agencies, and not the creditor to whom the debt may be owed. While the creditor cannot harass you, he is not subject to the same regulations as collection agencies. (Several states regulate the activities of creditors as well.)

A Collection Agency representative should not lead you to believe in any manner that he is a law enforcement officer or a representative of any governmental agency.

A debt collector cannot falsely represent himself or imply in any way that he is an officer of the court or that he is in any way affiliated with a law enforcement agency. A debt collector is prohibited from using a police badge or other symbol of authority. If you are contacted by a debt collector using these tactics, make sure you get his name and place of employment to use in any action against him.

A Collection Agency representative must not use or threaten force, violence, or other criminal means to harm you, your reputation, or property.

A debt collector is prohibited from using violence or threatening you physically, your reputation or your property to collect a debt. If a debt collector threatens to cause you harm you should, if possible, record the conversation and advise the collector that you are doing so, or ask a friend to listen to the call on an extension phone. Some collection agencies record telephone conversations their collectors have with debtors in order to minimize these violations.

A Collection Agency representative must not communicate with other people (except your lawyer or a consumer reporting agency) about your account

without your prior consent except to the extent reasonably necessary to enforce a court order.

A debt collector is prohibited from violating your privacy. Therefore, by law he cannot discuss your debt with anyone other than you or someone authorized by you. If a collector violates this law, have the individual to whom the information was disclosed write down that information, sign it and have it notarized. You may then use this to support your complaint to the appropriate governmental office. You may also have a claim for damages.

A Collection Agency representative must not communicate with you at any unusual time or place or at a time or place which the collector should know would be inconvenient to you. Unless the collector has knowledge of circumstances to the contrary, he should assume that the most convenient time for contacting you is between the hours of 8:00 a.m. and 9:00 p.m.

If the collector calls you before 8:00 a.m. and after 9:00 p.m. (unless he knows you have odd working hours, such as an evening shift, or that other unusual circumstances exist), he is violating the Fair Debt Collection Practices Act.

A debt collector should not contact you at your place of employment if he knows or has reason to know that your employer prohibits such calls.

If a collector contacts you at your place of employment, you can stop the calls by sending a letter to the collection agency advising the agency employees not to contact you at work. You should send this letter certified mail, return receipt requested, so the collection agency cannot dispute having received your letter.

If you tell the collector, in writing, that you refuse to pay the debt or that you want the collector to stop calling or contacting you, the collector should not communicate with you further except to:

- Advise you that he is stopping his efforts to collect the debt;
- Notify you that the collector or creditor may pursue other remedies ordinarily available, such as filing a lawsuit or notifying a credit reporting agency;
- Notify you that the collector or creditor will be taking a specific action regarding the debt, such as reporting it to the credit bureau.

> A Collection Agency representative must not communicate or threaten to communicate to anyone credit information about you which he knows or should know is false. If you are disputing the debt, any communication regarding the debt must also include the fact that you are disputing it.

If the collector talks to or otherwise communicates with anyone about your credit, he cannot by law give any information which he knows or should know is incorrect. If you do not agree with the collection agency regarding the debt and have notified the agency of your dispute, then that fact must also be included in any communication by the collector.

> A Collection Agency representative must not willfully communicate with you or any member of your family so frequently as could reasonably be expected to harass you or your family, or willfully engage in other conduct which can be reasonably be expected to annoy, abuse or harass you or any member of your family.

A debt collector cannot repeatedly call you on the telephone. If you get continuous telephone calls, you should keep track and write down the date and time of day for each call. To stop the continuous calls, write and send a letter to the agency, certified mail, return receipt requested, notifying the agency to stop contacting you. Once your letter is received by the agency, an agency collector is prohibited from contacting you again except to notify you that (a) contact will stop, or (b) that the agency is pursuing a specific remedy. A specific remedy might be that your debt will be assigned to a credit reporting agency.

> A Collection Agency representative shall not use profane, obscene, vulgar, or willfully abusive language in communicating with you or any member of your family.

If a debt collector uses profanity when calling you about payment of your debt, record the conversation, if possible, and let the collector know that the conversation is being recorded. Without the recording or some evidence of the language used, it is difficult to support your claim against the collector. You should also notify the creditor (the person to whom the debt was first owed) that the agency collector is using profanity in communications with you. The creditor might just recall your account (and other accounts) from the collection agency.

A Collection Agency representative must not, in order to embarrass or disgrace you, falsely represent or imply that you have committed a crime or other misconduct.

If the collector tells you that you have committed a crime, or that you are otherwise guilty of misconduct, ask him to explain the particular statute or law you have violated. Tell him he should provide you that information in writing (which is unlikely to happen). Keep track of your communication with the collector.

A Collection Agency representative must not use any written communication which appears to be a legal document or which gives the appearance of being authorized, issued or approved by a government, governmental agency, or attorney at law, when it is not—and must not misrepresent that documents ARE NOT legal or don't require a response from you when in fact they do.

A collection agency is prohibited from using any form of communication which may appear as though it came from an attorney's office, a governmental agency, or the police. This includes any document which looks like a court order, judgment or a subpoena.

On the other hand, if you do in fact receive a legal document, it is a violation of the law for the collector to mislead you into believing that it doesn't require any action.

A Collection Agency representative shall not communicate with you under the guise of an attorney by using the stationery of an attorney or forms or instruments which only attorneys are authorized to prepare.

A collection agency is prohibited from using a collection letter which falsely appears as though it was prepared by an attorney. A debt collector cannot send a collection letter from a "legal department" when no such department exists. If you have any doubt, ask to speak to the agency's attorney, and follow up with an inquiry to your local bar association. You should be able to ascertain whether or not the collection agency is trying to mislead you.

A Collection Agency representative shall not orally communicate with you in such a manner as to give the false impression or appearance that he is — or is associated with — an attorney.

If a debt collector calls and even implies that he is affiliated with an attorney, ask the collector to send you a letter on the attorney's stationery. If the collector has falsely stated or implied that he is associated with an attorney, he has violated this provision. (If possible, also record the conversation for future use—after you have told the collector that the conversation is being recorded.)

> **A Collection Agency representative must not advertise or threaten to advertise your account for sale in an effort to force you to pay, or falsely tell you that the account has been sold to a third party.**

A debt collector is prohibited from advertising or threatening to advertise your account for sale to a third party. The collector is also prohibited from falsely representing or implying that the account has been turned over to a third party.

> **A Collection Agency representative must not publish or post or threaten you that he will publish or post, individual names or any list of names of consumers, commonly known as a "deadbeat list," for the purpose of enforcing or attempting to enforce collection of your debt.**

Publishing your name as a debtor to force you into paying a debt is prohibited. If a collector threatens to place your name on a "deadbeat list" or in any manner make your debt public information, ask that the collector so notify you in writing. If you receive such a letter, or have knowledge that collector has in fact published your name, you may have a claim for damages.

> **A Collection Agency representative must not refuse to provide adequate identification of himself or his employer or other entity whom he represents when you ask him to do so**

A debt collector must give you his correct name and the correct name of his company when asked. Ask the collector to send you a statement on his company's letterhead containing his signature.

> **A Collection Agency representative must not mail any communication to you in an envelope or post card with words typed, written, or printed on the outside of the envelope or post card calculated to embarrass you.**

A debt collector is prohibited from mailing you an envelope or postcard which is intended to embarrass you into paying the debt. This includes language such as to "Deadbeat John Doe." If you receive correspondence which implies that you owe an outstanding debt, you may have a claim for damages.

Collectors are also prohibited from making false misrepresentations or implying that they either are, or work for, a consumer reporting agency (although some collection agencies are in fact affiliated or associated with reporting agencies).

It is considered an unfair practice for a collector to collect or attempt to collect any amount not specifically spelled out in the agreement creating the debt. (For example, interest can't be charged unless you initially agreed to pay it when you incurred the debt.)

Accepting checks postdated more than five days is prohibited unless the collection agency notifies you no more than ten and no less than three days before that the check will be deposited.

A collection agency cannot cause you to be charged with any expenses, such as collect telephone calls, without first disclosing to you the reason for the call.

A collection agency cannot falsely threaten to take your property if it has no authority or intent to do so or if the property is exempt (see Chapter 14).

If You Have an Attorney

If you have employed an attorney, you must provide the collection agency with the attorney's name and address. The agency must then send all correspondence directly to the attorney, and not to you.

What You Can Do On Your Own

The more knowledgeable you are about what a collection agency can and cannot do, the better equipped you will be to fight back. When contacted by a collection agency representative, keep track of the methods used to contact you, including the dates, times and places. If at all possible, have a witness. If you believe that a collection agency has violated any of the above laws, you have several options.

You should make it clear to the collection agency representative that you are aware of the laws, and believe they have been violated.

You may file a lawsuit for the amount of actual damages you have suffered, and additional damages up to $1,000.00. In assessing your damages, the court will consider the frequency and persistence of the violations by the debt collector, the nature of the violations, and the extent to which they were intentional. If you are successful, you will also be entitled to your court costs and attorneys fees. However, that the collector may not be held liable if he can prove to the court that the violation was not intentional and resulted from an honest mistake.

In one Texas case in 1995, a jury awarded a couple $11 million in a lawsuit against a credit card company for the abusive practices of its collection agency in attempting to collect a $2,000 debt. Collectors had made repetitious phone calls and used profanity, called the debtor's office 36 times in one hour, threatened to disrupt the debtor's work with bomb threats, and threatened to have them killed.

In any legal action by a collection agency to collect a debt, you can use a violation of the Fair Debt Collection Practices Act as a defense.

You may file a complaint with your state Attorney General's office (or the particular government office in your state which handles collection agencies—often a consumer affairs office). (See Appendix B.) You may also register a complaint with the office of the Federal Trade Commission nearest you.

Finally, if you truly owe the debt and the debt collector is making legitimate, legal contact, remember that most agencies will be willing to work with you in your efforts to clear up past-due accounts. If you tell the collector that you simply are unable to pay the entire balance due, you should be able to reach an agreeable payment plan or pay a lump-sum reduced amount. Remember, it is in the agency's interest to get money in as quickly as possible. A reduced lump-sum total payment may be much more attractive than small payments extended over a long period of time.

For Further Research

The Fair Debt Collection Practices Act is found in United States Code, Title 15, Sections 1692, 1692(a), 1692(b) "Acquisition of location information," 1692(c) "Communication in connection with debt collection," 1692(d) "Harassment or abuse," 1692(e) "False or misleading representations," 1692(f) "Unfair practices," 1692(g) "Validation of debts," and 1692(j) "Furnishing certain deceptive forms." Other sections of the Act include the legal actions which can be taken by debt collectors, civil liability of the collectors, and enforcement. You should also contact your state consumer affairs office for additional information. (See Appendix B.)

Sample Letters

July 21, 1996

EZ Collections   CERTIFIED MAIL
123 Short Street   RETURN RECEIPT REQUESTED
Anytown, USA   P-284-398-992

   RE: Account No. 298955-3018

Dear Sir or Madam:

Please do not contact me anymore regarding
the above-referenced debt.

                    Sincerely,

                    Jane Doe

July 21, 1996

EZ Collections   CERTIFIED MAIL
123 Short Street   RETURN RECEIPT REQUESTED
Anytown, USA   P-284-398-993

   RE: Account No. 298955-3018

Dear Sir or Madam:

I am disputing the validity of the above-
referenced debt for the following reason:

My account with Dr. Painless was paid in full
on August 31, 1990.

                         Sincerely,

                         Jane Doe

Two other examples of reasons for disputing:

"I have never had work done by ABC Drain
Cleaners."

"The service provided by Mr. Smith was
inadequate and not as represented by him."

August 2, 1996

Federal Trade Commission
1718 Peachtree St., N.W., Room 1000
Atlanta, GA 30367

        RE: EZ Collections
              123 Short Street
              Anytown, USA

Dear Sir or Madam:

On July 19, 1996, I received a letter from
EZ Collections claiming I owed $50.00 to a
Dr. Payne. I received a telephone call from
an EZ Collections employee on July 20, 1996,
demanding payment of the $50.00.

I then wrote to EZ Collections, stating that
I do not know a Dr. Payne, that I was never
a patient of his, and that I do not owe the
$50.00.

The EZ Collections employee continued to
call me and demand payment, often late at
night (after 9:00 p.m.).

I am hereby making a complaint against EZ
Collections for violating the Fair Debt
Collection Practices Act.

                              Sincerely,

                              Jane Doe
cc: EZ Collections

Chapter 4
Consumer Reporting Agencies and Your Credit Report

What is a Consumer Reporting Agency?

The Fair Credit Reporting Act (Public Law 91-508) regulates the activities of credit reporting agencies. A credit reporting agency, also known as a credit bureau and called "consumer reporting agency" under this law, means any person or business which assembles or evaluates consumer credit information for the purpose of providing consumer reports (commonly known as "credit reports") to third parties. Under the Fair Credit Reporting Act, "consumer" means an individual. You, as the person whose credit is being reported, are the consumer.

Information a Consumer Reporting Agency May Furnish

A reporting agency may furnish your credit report only under circumstances provided for by law, which are the following:
1. In response to a court order;
2. In accordance with written instructions from the consumer;
3. To any person which the reporting agency has reason to believe:
   a. intends to use the information in connection with a credit transaction involving the consumer on whom the information is to be furnished and involving the extension of credit to, or review or collection of an account of, the consumer; or

b.   intends to use the information for employment purposes; or

c.   intends to use the information in connection with the underwriting of insurance involving the consumer; or

d.   intends to use the information in connection with a determination of the consumer's eligibility for a license or other benefit granted by a governmental instrumentality required by law to consider an applicant's financial responsibility or status; or

e.   otherwise has a legitimate business need for the information in connection with a business transaction involving the consumer.

Obtaining Information From the Agency's Files

The contents of your credit report can affect your ability to get a loan as well as employment.   As a consumer, upon request and proper identification, you have the right to obtain the following information in the reporting agency's files:

1.   The nature and substance of all information (except medical information) in the agency's file on the consumer at the time of the request;

2.   The sources of the information (except as to information acquired solely for use in preparing an investigative consumer report and used for no other purpose, which is beyond the scope of this book);

3.   The recipients of any consumer report on the consumer which the reporting agency has furnished:

a.   for employment purposes within the two-year period preceding the request, and

b.   for any other purpose within the six-month period preceding the request.

The agency is required to provide you the requested information during normal business hours and on reasonable notice. The information should be provided to you in person if you have proper identification, or by telephone if you have made written request and have proper identification. If long distance, you must pay for the call. The agency must have trained personnel explain to you any questions you have about the report. If you make the request in person and have someone with you, the agency must have written permission from you to disclose any information in your companion's presence.

Items Your Report Cannot Contain

By law, your report cannot contain any of the following:
1. A discharge or final order in Bankruptcy Court dated more than ten years prior to the date of the credit report.
2. Lawsuits and judgments entered more than seven years prior to the date of the credit report. (However, if the applicable statute of limitations is longer than seven years, lawsuits and judgments may stay on the credit report until the applicable statute of limitations expire. For example, if your state allows a judgment to remain in effect for a period of ten years, then the ten-year period may apply, instead of the seven-year period.)
3. Paid tax liens which, from the date of payment, precede the report by more than seven years.
4. Accounts placed for collection or charged to profit and loss by the creditor which are dated more than seven years before the credit report.
5. Records of arrest, indictment, or conviction of crime which, from date of disposition, release, or parole, precede the report by more than seven years.
6. Any other adverse information which precedes the report by more than seven years.

However, the above restrictions do not apply if the report is to be used in connection with:
1. a credit transaction involving, or which may reasonably be expected to involve, a principal amount of $50,000.00 or more;
2. the underwriting of life insurance involving, or which may reasonably be expected to involve, a face amount of $50,000.00 or more;
3. the employment of any individual at an annual salary which equals, or which may reasonably be expected to equal, $20,000.00 or more.

What to Do if You Dispute Items in Your Report

The information contained in credit reports is obtained from a variety of sources, including local court records and businesses who pay a fee to the credit bureau. If you dispute the accuracy of any of the information in your credit report, do the following:
1. If you dispute the completeness or accuracy of any item of information contained in your file, and you let the reporting agency know of your dispute, the agency must, within a reasonable period of time, reinvestigate and record the current status of that information unless it has reasonable grounds to

believe that your dispute is frivolous or irrelevant. If after the reinvestigation the information is found to be inaccurate or can no longer be verified by the agency, then the agency must promptly delete the information from your report. Contradictory information in the file cannot be used by the agency as reasonable grounds for believing your dispute is frivolous or irrelevant. (See sample letter at end of this chapter.)

2. If the reinvestigation does not resolve the dispute, you may file a brief statement setting forth the nature of the dispute. The agency may limit the statement to not more than one hundred words if agency personnel provide you with assistance in writing a clear summary of the dispute.

3. Whenever you file a statement of dispute, unless there are reasonable grounds for the agency to believe your statement is frivolous or irrelevant, the agency must clearly note in any subsequent report containing the information that it is disputed, and must provide either your statement or a clear and accurate summary of your statement.

> Example: John and Sandy made a loan application to purchase a new home. The credit report reflected non-payment of a doctor bill approximately a year previously. John and Sandy thought their insurance company had paid the outstanding bill, and immediately made arrangements to pay once they realized this reflected negatively on their credit report. They also sent a letter to the reporting agency clarifying the reason for non-payment and stating that acceptable arrangements had been made with the physician to pay the bill. They were then given the mortgage they had applied for.

4. Following the removal by the agency of any information which is found to be inaccurate or whose accuracy can no longer be verified, or any notation in the agency's file as to disputed information, the agency must, at your request, (1) either furnish notification that the item has been deleted or (2) send the statement or summary regarding a disputed item to any person who is specifically designated by you and who has within two years prior received your credit report for employment purposes, or within six months previously received your credit report for any other purposes. The agency must clearly and conspicuously disclose to you your rights to make such a

request. The agency's disclosure must be made at or before the time the information is removed or your statement regarding the disputed information is received.

Cost of the Report

If you request a copy of your report within thirty days of notice from a collection agency affiliated with the reporting agency that your credit has been or may be adversely affected, or within thirty days of notice that employment is denied or credit or insurance rates are increased due to the report, then the report must be provided to you at no charge. Otherwise, after notifying you of the amount, the reporting agency may charge a reasonable fee for the report. The agency cannot charge for the deletion of any information which is determined to be inaccurate. Some agencies will provide you with one free copy per year. It may be a good idea for you to obtain a copy once a year to be sure of accuracy.

Reports for Employment Purposes

A reporting agency which furnishes a report for employment purposes that contains items of information which are matters of public record and are likely to have an adverse effect upon your ability to obtain employment **MUST:**

1. at the time such information is reported to a prospective employer, notify you of the fact that public record information is being reported by the consumer reporting agency, together with the name and address of the person to whom such information is being reported;
2. maintain strict procedures designed to insure that whenever public record information which is likely to have an adverse effect on your ability to obtain employment is reported, it is complete and up to date. Items relating to arrests, indictments, convictions, suits, tax liens, and outstanding judgments are considered up to date if the current public record status of the item at the time of the report is reported.

Requirements for Users of Reports

Whenever credit or insurance for personal, family or household purposes, or employment is denied or the charge for such credit or insurance is increased because of information contained in a report from a reporting agency, the user of the report must advise you and must supply the name and address of the consumer reporting agency making the report.

Use of Other Information

Whenever credit for personal, family or household purposes is denied or the charge for such credit is increased either wholly or in part because of information obtained from a person, other than a consumer reporting agency, which affects your credit worthiness, credit standing, credit capacity, character, general reputation, personal characteristics, or mode of living, the user of such information must, within a reasonable period of time after receiving your written request, disclose the nature of the information to you. The user must receive your written request within 60 days of your learning of the adverse action. At the time the user of the information tells you about the adverse action, he must also clearly and accurately disclose to you your right to make the written request.

Obtaining Information Under False Pretenses

Anyone who knowingly and willfully obtains information about a consumer from a reporting agency under false pretenses can be fined not more than $5,000 or imprisoned not more than one year, or both.

Providing Information to an Unauthorized Person

Any officer or employee of a reporting agency who knowingly and willfully provides information concerning an individual from the agency's files to a person *not authorized to receive that information* can be fined not more than $5,000 imprisoned not more than one year, or both.

Liability of Reporting Agency for Non-Compliance

Willful Non-Compliance. A reporting agency or user of information provided by a reporting agency which *willfully* fails to comply with the legal requirements is liable to you in an amount equal to the sum of:
1. any actual damages suffered by you as a result of the failure;
2. such amount of punitive damages as the court may allow; and
3. in the case of any successful action to enforce any liability under this section, the costs of the action together with reasonable attorney's fees as determined by the court.

Negligent Non-Compliance. A reporting agency or user of information provided by a reporting agency which *negligently* fails to comply with any requirement under the Consumer Credit Protection Act is liable to you in an amount equal to the sum of:

1.   any actual damages suffered by you as a result of the failure;
2.   in the case of any successful action to enforce any liability under the applicable section of the Act, the costs of the action together with reasonable attorney's fees as determined by the court.

Your Remedies. If you believe a credit reporting agency has failed to comply with any of the requirements under the Act, you may have recourse.

> Example: In one case consumers were awarded damages for embarrassment and humiliation as a result of a reporting agency's negligently furnishing an inaccurate mortgage report; in another, a consumer was awarded damages for mental anguish where he had to leave his employment numerous times to meet with the agency as a result of its refusal to disclose information to him about his credit report.

Time Limitations. You may bring an action against the agency within two years from the date on which the liability arises; *except,* where the agency has willfully misrepresented any information required to be disclosed and the information misrepresented is necessary to establish the agency's liability, the action may be brought within two years after discovery of the misrepresentation.

The Federal Trade Commission is the federal agency given the authority to enforce the provisions of the Fair Credit Reporting Act, and you may register a complaint at the office in your district. (See Appendix C.) You should send your complaint in writing, with a copy of the letter going to the credit reporting agency. (See sample letter at the end of this Chapter.)

For Further Research

The Federal Trade Commission Buyer's Guide No. 7, Fair Credit Reporting Act, contains a summary of this Act. You can find the Act in Title 15, United States Code, Chapter 41, Subchapter III. Refer to Sections 1681(a) through 1681(t). You should also contact your state's consumer affairs office for additional information.

Sample Letters

August 12, 1990

Credit Bureau   CERTIFIED MAIL
321 Broad Street RETURN RECEIPT REQUESTED
Your Town, USA   P-298-335-482

  RE: Credit Report for Jane Doe
     Social Security No 555-55-5555

Dear Sir or Madam:

On August, 1990, I was notified that credit had been denied me because of an entry on my credit report.

The credit report showed that I failed to make payment in the amount of $50.00 to a Dr. Payne. You must have me confused with another Jane Doe, as I do not know a Dr. Payne, nor have I ever used his services.

Please delete this entry from my credit report. Thank you.

       Sincerely,

       Jane Doe

August 12, 1990

Credit Bureau   CERTIFIED MAIL
321 Broad Street   RETURN RECEIPT REQUESTED
Your Town, USA   P-298-335-482

          RE: Credit Report for Jane Doe
                Social Security No 555-55-5555

Dear Sir or Madam:

In making application for a mortgage it
was brought to my attention that there is
an entry on my credit report showing that
I owe Dr. Feilgoodt a balance of $300.

The $300 was for medical treatment ap-
proximately one year ago. It was my
understanding that this amount had been
paid by my insurance company along with
other medical bills incurred at that
time. I did not receive a bill for this
amount after giving the medical center
business office information about my
insurance policy.

I intend to pay Dr. Feilgoodt's bill in
full as soon as possible. Please include
this letter in my credit report file.

Thank you.

                         Sincerely,

                         James Roe

August 12, 1990

Federal Trade Commission
1718 Peachtree St., N.W., Room 1000
Atlanta, GA   30367

        RE: Credit Bureau
              321 Broad Street
              Your Town, USA

Dear Sir or Madam:

On August 12, 1990, I notified Credit
Bureau, in writing, that an entry on my
credit report was incorrect, and asked
that it be deleted.

The credit report showed that I failed to
make payment in the amount of $50.00 to a
Dr. Payne. Apparently Credit Bureau has
me confused with another Jane Doe, as I
do not know a Dr. Payne, nor have I ever
used his services.

Credit Bureau refused to follow up on my
letter and the entry still shows on my
credit report without an explanation or
notice that it is disputed.

I wish to file a complaint against Credit
Bureau under the Fair Credit Reporting
Act.

                    Sincerely,

                    Jane Doe
cc: Credit Bureau

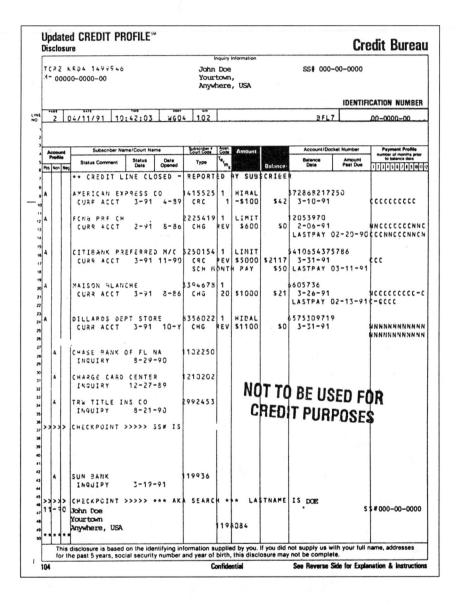

Sample "Credit Profile" or Credit Report as prepared by credit reporting agency.

Chapter 5
The Internal Revenue Service

Collection of Money Owed to the IRS

Unlike other creditors, the IRS has almost unlimited access to your property if you owe a tax bill. The IRS has the authority to take your house (homestead doesn't matter), your bank accounts, your wages, your business, and virtually anything else you own in order to pay outstanding taxes. As a practical matter, most debts can be worked out with an IRS agent, and a payment plan can be arranged. However, before you figure out how you're going to pay the bill, read on.

Don't Assume an IRS Bill is Correct

If you get a notice from the IRS stating that you miscalculated your taxes due and that you still owe money, don't panic. First, check the figures. It may well be that the IRS clerk checking your return did the miscalculation. In fact, it is possible that the amount the IRS claims you owe isn't actually due. During the busiest tax filing season the IRS hires temporary workers, and many of the full-time entry-level employees who first see your return are poorly trained. It's been estimated that nearly half of the official notices from the IRS demanding additional payments are inaccurate.

You may need help in your recalculations. If you find that the IRS has in fact made a mistake, respond to the notice, in writing, and enclose a copy of your calculations as well as a copy of the IRS notice.

Don't Leave an IRS Inquiry Unanswered

It is of utmost importance that you respond to an IRS inquiry no later than the due date which is written on their correspondence. If you ignore the IRS letters telling you that you owe additional taxes, you will be sent several statements, a "Notice of Deficiency" or a similar notice (depending upon the type of error the IRS claims you made) which gives you an opportunity to protest the IRS assessment by filing your protest in the U.S. Tax Court, and finally an "assessment notice," which advises you that liens are being filed against all of your property. These liens remain until the amount due is paid. If you don't respond this time, the IRS agent may begin taking your property after a 30-day waiting period.

Property the IRS Can Take for Taxes Due

The IRS has the right to take virtually all of your property without any regard to the equity (except as specifically set forth below.) The IRS agent can take your car, your house, bank accounts, and your wages.

The IRS can take your property, sell it for just enough to pay the taxes owed and the costs of the sale, without any consideration for the amount of equity you have in it.

Taxpayers Bill of Rights

Congress passed a Taxpayers Bill of Rights in 1990, to help people who for some reason are overwhelmed by the Internal Revenue Service. You can apply for a Taxpayer Assistance Order to Relieve Hardship (TAO) if you are in a position of extreme financial crisis, such as possible loss of a job or medical care. The TAO requires that IRS employees stop whatever action is being taken against you until the crisis is resolved. You can apply for a TAO by filing IRS Form 911. The form is available by calling 1-800-829-1040 and asking for a Problem Resolution Officer to review your case.

What the IRS Cannot Take

There are certain items the IRS by law cannot touch (26 USC Sec. 6334). These are:
- wearing apparel and such school books as are necessary for you or members of your family
- fuel, food, furniture and personal effects totalling $1,650.00 ($1,550 if levy issued in 1989) if you are head of a household (also may include arms for personal use, livestock and poultry)

- so many of the books and tools necessary for your trade, business or profession which do not exceed $1,100 total in value ($1,050 if levy issued in 1989)
- unemployment benefits
- mail addressed to any person (but not yet delivered)
- certain annuity and pension payments under the Railroad Retirement Act, benefits under the Railroad Unemployment Insurance Act, special pension payments received by a person whose name has been entered on the Army, Navy, Air Force and Coast Guard Medal of Honor roll and annuities based on retired or retainer pay
- workman's compensation benefits
- judgments for support of minor children (if you have been ordered to pay, the amount necessary for you to comply with judgment is exempt)
- minimum exemption for wages, salary, and other income calculated as the aggregate amount of the deductions for personal exemptions allowed in the tax year in which the tax levy occurs, divided by 52 (If you don't submit a written and verified statement to the IRS specifying the facts necessary to determine the proper amount, the exemption will be applied as if you were a married individual filing a separate return with only one exemption)
- certain service-connected disability payments
- certain public assistance payments
- assistance under the Job Training Partnership Act
- your principal residence may be exempt *unless* the district or assistant district IRS director approves the levy on your property *or* the Secretary of the IRS finds that collection of the tax is in jeopardy

IRS Time Limitations

The IRS can come after you for additional taxes only three years after you filed the return. However, if the IRS finds that the gross income shown on your return was 25 per cent less than the actual amount, the time limitation is increased to six years. If you failed to file or filed a fraudulent return, there is no time limitation.

If Your Tax Return is Audited

Every year a certain number of tax returns are chosen by the Internal Revenue Service for an audit. An audit simply means an official examination and verification of your financial accounts and records. A return may be selected for audit because of certain information it contains—such as deductions for home office expenses—or it may be a random selection. Audits are made by correspondence (you are asked to send in supporting evidence of figures), in an IRS examiner's office, or at your home or office.

To prepare for an audit of your tax return you should make sure that all your records are in order and that the figures on your tax return can be supported by documentation. In other words, if you have deducted costs for entertainment as a business expense, you should be able to clearly show the IRS examiner that the entertainment was in fact for a business purpose. Similarly, if you have deducted expenses for maintaining a portion of your home as an office, be able to show that the area is being used exclusively for your business.

You may want to have someone represent you at the audit—an accountant, your bookkeeper, or in some cases, an attorney—removing you from the immediate scrutiny and questioning of the examiner. You don't have to be physically present at the audit. Your representative can come back to you for clarification of any items questioned by the examiner and give you an opportunity to put some forethought into your response. If you do go alone and questions come up which you are unable to answer adequately, you can tell the examiner that you will have to consult with your accountant or other tax advisor.

Although the majority of audits do result in the taxpayer owing money, it isn't always the case. The important point to remember is to be prepared. Of course, preparation should begin long before you receive notice of an audit. Keep accurate records throughout each year which support the figures on your return and your audit should go smoothly. Finally, if the examiner's report shows that you owe additional tax, you'll have 30 days to accept or contest the decision.

What You Can Do

The first step, of course, is to file your tax returns (or request for extensions), on or before the IRS deadline. If you are charged a penalty for filing late, send a notarized statement and whatever documentation you have showing the date it was mailed. If you are filing late, include a letter and supporting evidence, if available, explaining why. The IRS examiner may accept the late filing without a penalty. Even if you have met the deadlines, it may not be enough. The IRS can come back to you for more money. This is done by sending you a letter stating that there is a deficiency in your tax payment.

- If you dispute a calculation, send a letter of explanation, including your calculation. Keep your letter short, simple, and to the point so it can be easily understood. The IRS notices usually come in duplicate, giving you the copy to use for your response. You should include this copy, and always reference the IRS file number on correspondence to make sure it doesn't get lost. You should send correspondence by certified mail, with a return receipt requested. This way, there can be no dispute by the IRS that they received your response.

- If you get further notices without any acknowledgment of the letter you sent, write again and include copies of all correspondence you already sent regarding that particular claim. If you still get another notice, contact the IRS Problem Resolution Officer nearest you. If you believe the IRS is beyond the time limitation, you can file a petition in the U.S. Tax Court to have the taxes, interest and penalties dropped. (See page 55.)

- If you owe the bill, negotiate with the IRS for a reduced lump-sum amount *or* arrange a payment plan. If you do set up a payment plan, make sure you keep the payments current. If you don't the IRS can take other action to collect.

- Consider taking out a loan from your bank or other source, if possible, and paying the IRS off. It may be better to owe money to the bank than to risk your house being seized by the IRS. This would also eliminate the IRS charge for penalties and interest. (If the IRS has waived penalties, or none are being charged, then a payment plan with the IRS might make better economic sense.)

- Finally, a bankruptcy filing will temporarily stop all actions by the IRS to collect unpaid taxes. However, bankruptcy will not discharge your debt to the IRS (unless the time limitation has expired *and* you have not had negotiations with the IRS or a tax court case determination within 240 days of filing the bankruptcy petition). A Chapter 13 filing will not discharge the debt for unpaid taxes, but will allow you to pay the entire amount due according to your repayment plan schedule.

For Further Research

The Internal Revenue Service list of exemptions is found in Title 12, United States Code, Chapter 64, Subtitle F - Collection, Section 6334.

IRS Publication 5, *Appeal Rights and Preparation of Protests for Unagreed Cases*, will help you understand your rights to appeal an examiner's decision if your return is audited.

IRS Publication 556, *Examination of Returns, Appeal Rights, and Claims for Refund*, will help you in understanding your rights to appeal an IRS decision in the courts.

IRS Publication 586A, *The Collection Process*, and Publication 594, *The Collection Process*, will help you understand your rights if the IRS attempts to collect unpaid taxes.

Sample IRS Correspondence

September 20, 1996

Internal Revenue Service   CERTIFIED MAIL
Atlanta, GA 39901   RETURN RECEIPT REQUESTED
                          P-288-398-487

    RE: Jane Doe
    Social Security No. 555-55-5555
    Your file reference no.95-34453

Dear Sir or Madam,

    I have received your letter of September 10, 1996, a copy of which is attached, advising me that I still owe $759.28.

    I have recalculated my 1989 tax return and come up with the same figures as before. My calculations are attached.

    Please correct your records and stop sending me notices, or explain specifically where and how the error is to be found.

    Thank you.

                    Sincerely,

                    Jane Doe

This letter should be sent in response to a notice of deficiency or a correction notice.

Sample Tax Case Petition Form

```
                        PETITION
                    (SMALL TAX CASE)
                UNITED STATES TAX COURT
Jane Doe,                           )
        Petitioner,                 )
                                    )
vs.                                 )         Docket No.
                                    )
Commissioner of Internal Revenue,   )
        Respondent.                 )
```

PETITION

1. Petitioner ask the Court to redetermine the tax deficiencies for the year <u>1995</u> as set forth in the Notice of Deficiency dated <u>September 10, 1996</u>, a copy of which is attached to this Petition. The Notice was issued by the Office of the Internal Revenue Service at <u>Atlanta, Georgia</u>.

2. Petitioner's taxpayer identification number (social security number) is <u>555-55-5555</u>.

3. Petitioner makes the following claim(s) regarding his/their tax liability:

Year	Amount of Deficiency Disputed	Addition to Tax (Penalty) Disputed	Amount of Over-payment Claim
1995	$759.28	$113.90	-0-

4. Those adjustments or changes in the Notice of Deficiency with which Petitioners disagrees and why: The IRS has failed to show where any errors were made in the Petitioner's tax return as originally filed.

Petitioner requests that the proceedings in this case be conducted as a "Small Tax Case" under Section 7463 of the Internal Revenue Code of 1954, as amended, and Rule 172 of the Rules of Practice and Procedure of the United States Tax Court. A decision in a "Small Tax Case" is final and cannot be appealed by either party.

```
                        _____
                        Signature of Petitioner
                        447 Tea Party Lane
                        Clearwater, FL  34617
                        (813) 555-5555
```

Chapter 6
Loan Disclosure Requirements — Truth in Lending

The Federal Law

Although the text of the Federal Consumer Credit Protection Act ("Act") is too extensive and complex to recite in this book, it is important for you to know that you have the right to certain information about a loan given to you by a lender or creditor.

Congress passed the "Consumer Credit Protection Act" to assure that every creditor who, in the ordinary course of business, regularly extends or offers to extend or arrange for the extension of consumer credit, gives meaningful information regarding the cost of the credit and other relevant information so that you may readily compare the various credit terms available to you from different sources and avoid the uninformed use of credit. You should have the benefit of sufficient information about the proposed loan so that you can make an informed decision as to whether you want to accept the terms. If you have not had the benefit of all the information which the law requires be given to you, then you may have the basis for a lawsuit against the creditor, or you may have a counterclaim if the creditor sues you for non-payment.

The Consumer Credit Protection Act includes the Truth in Lending regulations (also known as Regulation Z), which set forth the rules lenders must comply with when they give you credit. It gives you the right to cancel certain credit transactions which involve a lien on your residence. It also gives you certain legal rights if the lender has misrepresented a loan to you, or has failed to make all the disclosures accurately as required under the Act. (The Act requires disclosure in other consumer credit transactions, as well as leases and credit cards, which will be discussed in Chapters 7 and 8.)

Required Disclosures

The disclosures that must be made by a lender include:
1. The identity of the creditor (lender);
2. The amount financed, which is the amount of credit of which the borrower has actual use;
3. Along with the disclosure of the amount financed, a lender must provide a statement of your right to obtain, upon a written request, a written itemization of the amount financed (which must then be furnished);
4. The finance charge;
5. The finance charge expressed as an annual percentage rate;
6. The number, amount, and due dates or period of payments scheduled to repay the total loan;
7. Where the lender is also the seller, the total of the cash price of the property and the finance charge;
8. Descriptive explanations of the terms "amount financed," "finance charge," "annual percentage rate," "total of payments," and "total sale price." The descriptive explanation of "total sale price" must include a reference to the amount of the downpayment;
9. Where credit is secured, as with a mortgage, a statement that a security interest has been taken in either (a) the property which is purchased as part of the credit transaction, or (b) property not purchased as part of the credit transaction identified by item or type;
10. Any dollar charge or percentage amount which may be imposed by a creditor solely on account of a late payment, other than a deferral or extension charge;
11. A statement as to whether or not you are entitled to a rebate of any finance charge upon refinancing or prepayment in full, if the obligation involves a precomputed finance charge. A statement whether or not there will be a penalty imposed in those same circumstances if the obligation involves a finance charge computed from time to time by application of a rate to the unpaid principal balance.
12. A statement that you should refer to the appropriate contract document for any information that document provides about nonpayment, default, the right to accelerate the maturity of the debt, and prepayment rebates and penalties.

13. In any residential mortgage transaction, a statement indicating whether someone who buys the property from you may assume the debt obligation on its original terms and conditions.

Errors by the creditor in the Truth in Lending Disclosures are usually not brought to the creditor's attention by the borrower until the creditor tries to collect the debt. If the creditor finds an error before any default in payment, the creditor will probably prepare new documents with the correct information (See page 62.)

Time Periods in Which Disclosures Must be Made

Telephone Orders

If you place a purchase order by mail or telephone without being personally solicited by the creditor, and the cash price and total sale price and the terms of financing, including the annual percentage rate, are set forth in the creditor's catalog or other printed material distributed to the public, then the required disclosures may be made by the creditor at any time not later than the first payment due date.

Loan Requests by Telephone

If you make a request for a loan by mail or telephone and the creditor has not personally solicited you, and the terms of financing, including the annual percentage rate for representative amounts of credit are set forth in the creditor's printed material distributed to the public or in the loan contract or other printed material delivered to you, then the disclosures must be made no later than the date the first payment is due.

If the creditor personally solicits you in either case, the disclosures must be made *before* you obligate yourself to the creditor.

Purchasing in a Series

If your purchase is one of a series according to an agreement providing that the deferred payment price of a particular sale be added to the existing outstanding balance, and you have already agreed to the annual percentage rate and finance charge, and the creditor isn't retaining a security interest in any of the property you've purchased, then the disclosure may be made any time before the first payment is due.

Finance Charge and Annual Percentage Rate (APR)

Regulation Z spells out exactly how the finance charge and annual percentage rate on your loan are to be determined, and how these and other charges related to your loan are to be disclosed to you. The manner in which these calculations are made is determined by federal statute and by the Board of Governors of the Federal Reserve System ("Board").

Finance Charge

In determining whether a lender has given you all the required information about your loan, one of the most important items for you to review is the finance charge. The finance charge is determined as the sum of all charges, payable directly or indirectly by the borrower, and imposed directly or indirectly by the creditor as an incident to the extension of credit. The following charges are examples of costs included in the finance charge:

1. Interest and any amount payable under a point, discount, or other system of additional charges;
2. Service or carrying charge;
3. Loan fee, finder's fee, or similar charge;
4. Fee for an investigation or credit report;
5. Premium or other charge for any guarantee or insurance protecting the creditor against the obligor's default or other credit loss.

Example: A buyer of a food freezer was required to purchase a freezer service policy to assure repair of the freezer for the duration of the period over which the buyer agreed to make installment payments. The charge for the service policy was added to the sale price and included in the amount financed, but not disclosed to the buyer. The cost of the freezer service policy was a "finance charge," the disclosure of which was required by law. The seller was liable for damages to the buyer.

In deciding whether an item must be included in the finance charge, the important question is whether the lender refuses to extend credit until you agree to pay the charge. If a charge is not itemized and disclosed by the lender, it still needs to be included in the computation of the finance charge, even if the charge is not a charge for credit.

Annual Percentage Rate

The APR simply reflects the cost of your loan as a yearly rate. This figure must be disclosed to you, because it will usually be higher than the interest rate you are paying on your note. Borrowers often wonder whether the bank has increased the interest rate quoted to them. The difference between the interest rate quoted and stated on your promissory note and the interest rate (APR) shown on the disclosure form is due to difference in calculations. There are several methods of determining the annual percentage rate (APR) applied to your loan. The most important point to remember is that any prepaid finance charges are considered a reduction in the principal amount of the loan.

> **Example:** If you borrow $10,000.00 at 10% interest for one year, and the bank deducts $300.00 in loan closing costs from the $10,000.00 and you must make up the difference, then you have actually only received $9,700.00. The total of 10% interest on $10,000.00, or $1,000.00, is $11,000.00. This is the amount you will pay according to your loan. However, because of the deduction of closing costs, the bank is actually giving you only $9,700.00. The total of $11,000.00 you will pay is actually $9,700.00 at 13.40 per cent interest.

Remember that any income which the bank earns as the result of your loan is to be considered a finance charge, including such items as a bank appraisal fee, document preparation fee, points, origination fee, etc. These charges should be considered a reduction in the principal amount of the loan.

The lender will take three variables into consideration in computing the APR: 1) the number of payments to be made over the complete term of the loan (usually 360 for a real estate loan), 2) the interest rate, and 3) the principal balance remaining to be paid on the loan after deducting those items which are prepaid finance charges. The fourth variable, the total of the periodic (monthly) payments (principal and interest), will then be computed. A rough approximation of the calculation is as follows: first the finance charge to be paid over the term of the loan is totalled (in a real estate loan, the monthly finance charge will vary according to an amortization schedule); second, this total is then divided by the number of years of the loan; and third, this figure is then again divided by the total amount financed (including the principal amount of the loan and reflecting any finance charges). **NOTE: This is a complicated calculation, and is not to be attempted arithmetically, but should be reviewed by someone competent and experienced in applying the Regulation Z requirements.**

An APR on an open-end (equity line) loan is calculated as if the loan were carried out to full term at the highest interest rate.

All items required to be disclosed must be disclosed clearly, conspicuously, and in meaningful sequence. The terms "annual percentage rate" and "finance charge" must be disclosed more conspicuously than other terms or information provided in connection with a transaction, except information relating the identity of the creditor. (See Page 67 at the end of this Chapter.) The disclosures must be made to the person who is to be obligated on the loan. (If you are taking out the loan, with your father's advice, then the disclosures must be made to you— making them to your father is not sufficient.)

(Although beyond the scope of this book, you should also note that banks and other real estate lenders are required to follow the Federal Real Estate Settlement Procedures Act of 1974 "RESPA" which regulates settlement of a residential loan transaction. For information about RESPA, write to the U.S. Department of Housing and Urban Development, Director, Office of Insured Single Family Housing, Attention: RESPA, 451 Seventh St., S.W., Washington, D.C. 20410. For information regarding manufactured home financing requirements, contact the Office of Manufactured Housing and Regulatory Functions, 451 Seventh Street, S.W., Washington, D.C.)

Good Faith Estimate — Residential Mortgages

In a residential mortgage transaction, the lender must make a good faith estimate of the disclosures required under Regulation Z *before* the credit is extended, or the lender must either deliver or place the estimate in the mail to the borrower *no later than three business days* after the lender receives the borrower's written application, whichever date is earlier. If the good faith estimate contains an annual percentage rate which is subsequently determined to be inaccurate by the acceptable calculations, then the lender must furnish another good faith estimate at the time of settlement (when the loan is actually made and documents signed). (See page 68 for sample of Good Faith Estimate.)

Equity Line Mortgages and Your Right to Rescind

If you have borrowed funds for purposes other than the purchase of your principal residence, and the lender has taken an interest in your residence as collateral for the loan, the law requires that you be given a three-day right of rescission. In other words, you have until midnight of the third business day following the date of signing the loan documents or receipt of the all required disclosures to cancel the loan. However, you must notify the creditor by mail, telegram, or other writing of your cancellation.

Every joint owner who will be obligated to pay back the loan has the right to receive the disclosures and must be given a notice of the right to cancel. (See page 70.)

Release from your obligations

When you exercise your right to rescind, you are not liable for any finance or other charge, and any security interest the creditor may have in your property becomes void. Within twenty days after you exercise your right to rescind, the creditor must return to you any money or property given as earnest money, downpayment, or otherwise, and must take any action required to reflect the termination of any security interest the creditor may have acquired as a result of the transaction.

Property to be returned to creditor

As the borrower you must also return to the creditor, within a reasonable time period after you rescind the transaction, any funds or value the creditor has advanced to you. However, if the creditor fails to return the property required to be returned to you, then you have no further obligation to return the funds to the creditor.

If the creditor fails to take the property

If the creditor does not take possession of the property within ten days of the date you offer, you may be entitled to keep the property. (In most cases this would involve a return of the principal amount loaned to you by the creditor.) A court can refuse your request to have the transaction rescinded if you fail to return any loan proceeds advanced to you by the lender.

Loans not affected by right of rescission

The right of rescission does not apply to:
(a) a residential mortgage transaction in which the funds are used to purchase the property;
(b) a transaction which constitutes the refinancing or consolidation (with no new advances) of the principal balance then due and any accrued and unpaid finance charges of an existing extension of credit by the same creditor, secured by an interest in the same property;
(c) a transaction in which an agency of a State is a creditor; or
(d) advances under a preexisting open end credit plan if a security interest has already been retained or acquired by the lender and such advances are in accordance with a previously established credit limit for such plan.

If the lender fails to provide you with the information required to be disclosed, you have three years from the date of the conclusion of the transaction or when you sell the property, whichever comes first, to rescind the transaction. If the creditor fails to disclose required information, you are not limited by the normal three-day rescission period.

Balloon Payments on Consumer Loans

Some states prohibit balloon payments on consumer loans for family or household purposes; others require that you be given the right to refinance the loan when the balloon payment comes due. (A balloon payment is the amount due at the end of a loan term after you have made regular, smaller payments for a period of time.) Your state Attorney General's office or the consumer office should have information regarding balloon payments on consumer loans.

Refinancing

If any existing extension of credit is refinanced, or two or more existing extensions of credit are consolidated, or an existing obligation is increased, these will be considered new transactions subject to the disclosure requirements of the Act. If your loan has been refinanced or the terms have otherwise changed, determine whether your lender gave you all the required information.

When Disclosure is Not Required

The disclosure requirements described above do not apply to the following transactions:
  (1) Credit transactions involving extensions of credit primarily for business, commercial, or agricultural purposes, or to government or governmental agencies, or to organizations.
  (2) Transactions in securities or commodities accounts by a broker-dealer registered with the Securities and Exchange Commission.
  (3) Credit transactions, other than those in which a security interest is or will be acquired in real property, or in personal property used or expected to be used as the principal dwelling of the consumer, in which the total amount financed exceeds $25,000.00.
  (4) Transactions under public utility tariffs, if the Board determines that a State regulatory body regulates the charges for the public utility services involved, the charges for delayed payment, and any discount allowed for early payment.

The Act covers consumer credit transactions primarily for personal, family, household, or agricultural purposes.

Lenders' Liabilities and Your Rights and Obligations

The creditor has no liability if, within sixty days of discovering an error and before receiving notice from you of the error, the creditor notifies you and makes the appropriate adjustments to make sure that you will not be required to pay an amount greater than the charge actually disclosed, or the dollar equivalent of the annual percentage rate actually disclosed, whichever is lower.

The creditor will not be held liable if the creditor shows that the violation was not intentional and resulted from an honest error, including clerical or computer malfunction. However, an error of legal judgment with respect to a person's obligations is not considered an honest error. In most real estate loan transactions with a commercial lender you will be asked to sign a document that says you agree to cooperate if a correction is required due to a clerical error. (See page 69.)

You have no legal right to offset any amount which the creditor may owe you against any other amount you owe the creditor, unless you have a court judgment against the creditor. However, you should assert the creditor's violation of the Act as a defense against any legal action to collect a debt brought by a creditor who is in violation of the Act. *In a real estate foreclosure action, Regulation Z may be your strongest defense.* Considering the volume of paperwork required in a loan transaction and the number of transactions a commercial lender may make, it is possible that an error was made. You should get a copy of all the disclosure documents related to your loan. You should then review them carefully with someone who fully understands the disclosure requirements and the calculations. If there is a possibility of an error, it may be wise for you to hire an attorney to review the documents and give you an opinion as to whether you should proceed legally against the lender. (Even if ultimately the court doesn't agree that the lender violated the Act, using this as a defense will delay the lender's lawsuit, including a foreclosure action.) Remember that, if you are successful in a lawsuit against a creditor who violated any provisions of the Act, your attorneys fees and costs must be paid by the creditor.

For any violation of the Act, a creditor may be liable to you in an amount equal to:

(1) any actual damage suffered by you as a result of the failure to disclose all of the information required;

(2) twice the amount of any finance charge in connection with the transaction;

(3) the reasonable attorneys fees and costs incurred in a successful legal action.

In 1994 a federal court ruled that homeowners can break their mortgages if they can prove that their lender violated truth in lending rules. Since then some lawyers have been trying to start class action lawsuits against lenders and have been seeking out people who want to sue. However, the bankers' powerful lobby in Congress is trying to pass a law to block such lawsuits, claiming they could cost them $220 billion. If you think you might have such a claim, you should seek out an attorney in your area who specializes in consumer or banking law to see if he or she might take your case.

For Further Research

If you need additional information regarding Regulation Z, you may write to the Division of Consumer and Community Affairs, Board of Governors of the Federal Reserve System, Washington, D.C. 20551 or to your regional Federal Trade Commission office, Division of Credit Practices-Bureau of Consumer Affairs. (See Appendix C). The text of the Act is contained in Title 15, United States Code, Chapter 41, Subchapter I, Consumer Credit Cost Disclosure, Sections 1601 through 1635. The regulations enforcing the Act are found in the "Truth in Lending Regulations," Title 12, Banks & Banking, Part 226.

Truth in Lending Disclosure Statement

On the following page is a sample "Truth in Lending Disclosure Statement." The box titled "Annual Percentage Rate" may be different from the rate quoted to you at the time of your mortgage application, and may be different from the interest rate you were promised. This rate should reflect any prepaid costs or items included in the financing. For example, the rate shown is 9.65%. The rate the borrower is paying on an $80,000.00 loan is 9.25%. The promissory note will show $80,000.00 to be paid back at 9.25% interest. Take the $80,000.00, less $2,728.00 in total closing costs (these include $800 in origination fee, $1600 discount points, $113 appraisal fee, $50 credit report, and $165 underwriting fee). The remaining amount is $77,272.00. The $77,272.00, with the payments calculated on the $80,000.00 amount, comes to 9.65% annual percentage rate.

The box titled "Finance Charge" shows the total amount of interest you will be paying over the total term of the loan.

The box titled "Amount Financed" is somewhat less than the amount of the mortgage because the prepaid costs have been deducted, as described in above.

The box titled "Total of Payments" is the total of the figures in the previous two boxes, representing the total amount which you will be paying if you pay the full term of the loan.

Sample Disclosure Form

FEDERAL TRUTH IN LENDING DISCLOSURE/REDISCLOSURE STATEMENT

Creditor: Your Bank, USA

Borrower(s): Jane & Joe Doe

Account Number: 000-00000-00

ANNUAL PERCENTAGE RATE The cost of your credit as a yearly rate	FINANCE CHARGE The dollar amount the credit will cost you	Amount Financed The amount of credit provided to you or on your behalf	Total of Payments The amount you will have paid after you have made all payments as scheduled
9.65 %	$ 159,658.72 ●	$ 77,272.00	$ 236,930.72

Your payment schedule will be:

NUMBER OF PAYMENTS	AMOUNT OF PAYMENTS	WHEN PAYMENTS ARE DUE
359	$ 658.14	Monthly Beginning 08/01/91
1	658.45	07/01/21

Variable Rate: ☐ If checked, your loan contains a variable-rate feature. Disclosures about the variable-rate feature have been provided to you earlier.

Demand Feature: ☐ If checked, this obligation has a demand feature.

Insurance: You may obtain property insurance from anyone you want that is acceptable to the Creditor. ☒ If checked, you can get insurance from and you will pay $ 400.00 ● for 12 months coverage.

Security: You are giving a security interest in: ☐ property being purchased ☒ property located at

Late Charges: If a payment is late, you will be charged 5 % of the payment.

Prepayment: If you pay off early, you ☐ may ☒ will not have to pay a penalty. You ☐ may ☒ will not be entitled to a refund of part of the finance charge .

Assumption: Someone buying your house ☐ may, subject to conditions be allowed to ☒ cannot assume the remainder of the mortgage on the original terms.

See your contract documents for any additional information about nonpayment, default, any required repayment in full before the scheduled date, prepayment refunds and penalties and assumption policy.

● means an estimate

ACKNOWLEDGMENT

By signing below you acknowledge that you have received a completed copy of this Federal Truth in Lending Statement prior to the execution of any closing documents.

_____   _____
Date of Acknowledgment   Borrower

_____   _____
Date of Acknowledgment   Borrower

Sample Good Faith Estimate

COPY

GOOD FAITH ESTIMATE OF SETTLEMENT CHARGES

PROPERTY ADDRESS: _____

SALES PRICE $ __Refinance__   LOAN REQUEST $ __40,000.00__   INT. RATE __9.90%__ TERM __180 Mos.__

ITEMS PAYABLE IN CONNECTION WITH LOAN   Fixed   15 Yrs.

801	Loan Origination Fee __1.0__ %	400.00	**ESTIMATED MONTHLY PAYMENTS**
802	Loan Discount Fee __.25__ %	100.00	Prin. & Int. — 427.40
803	Appraisal Fee	225.00	Taxes — 78.00
804	Credit Report	45.00	Ins. — -0-
805	Lenders Inspection Fee	-0-	PMI Ins. — -0-
901	Prepaid Interest (4/26/91–5/1/91)	54.25	Maint. Fee — -0-
902	Mortgage Ins. Premium	-0-	TOTAL PAYMENT — 505.40
1107	Attorney's Fees	-0-	**DETAILS OF PURCHASE**
1108	Title Insurance	345.00*	a. Purchase Price $
1201	Recording Fees .32¢	24.00	b. Total Closing Costs (Est.) $ 1,467.75
1202	Doc Stamps (15¢ per $100)	128.00	c. Prepaid Escrows (Est.) $ 546.00
1203	Int. Tax (20¢ per $100)	80.00	d. Total (a + b + c) $ 2,013.75
1301	Survey	-0-	e. Amount This Mortgage (40,000.00)
1302	Pest Inspection	-0-	f. Other Financing ( )
1303	Tax Service Fee	66.50	g. Other Equity ( )
1304	Warehouse Fee	-0-	h. Amount of Cash Deposit ( )
1305	Other	-0-	i. Closing Costs Paid by Seller ( )
1400	**TOTAL SETTLEMENT CHARGES**	1,467.75	j. Cash Reqd. For Closing (Est.) $

☐ The items marked by an * are based upon charges for services provided by:

NAME _____

ADDRESS _____

_____

TELEPHONE _____

Escrows – Real Estate Taxes

Escrow 7 Months – Nov. to May
$78 @ Month x 7 = $546.00

This provider ☐ does ☐ does not have a business relationship with the Lender.
THIS FORM DOES NOT COVER ALL ITEMS YOU WILL BE REQUIRED TO PAY IN CASH AT SETTLEMENT, FOR EXAMPLE DEPOSITS IN ESCROW FOR REAL ESTATE TAXES AND INSURANCE, YOU MAY WISH TO INQUIRE AS TO THE AMOUNTS OF SUCH ITEMS. YOU MAY BE REQUIRED TO, PAY OTHER ADDITIONAL AMOUNTS AT SETTLEMENT.
     We request that the estimated fee of $_____ for an appraisal and $_____ for a credit report be prepaid at the time of application since these are costs connected with your loan request that must be paid as we are billed. These fees are considered non-refundable.

NOTE: The above Good Faith Estimate of Settlement Charges are made pursuant to the requirements of the Real Estate Settlement Procedures Act (RESPA). The figures are estimates only, and the actual charges due at settlement may be different.

I hereby acknowledge receipt of a fully completed copy of this "Good Faith Estimate of Settlement Charges" along with a copy of the HUD Booklet.

_____   _____
DATE   BORROWER

_____   _____
DATE   CO-BORROWER

Sample Compliance Agreement

STATE OF
COUNTY OF

BORROWERS:

LENDER:

PROPERTY LEGAL:

COMPLIANCE AGREEMENT

THE UNDERSIGNED BORROWER(S) FOR AND IN CONSIDERATION OF THE ABOVE REFERENCED
LENDER THIS DATE FUNDING THE CLOSING OF THIS LOAN AGREES, IF REQUESTED BY
LENDER OR CLOSING AGENT FOR LENDER, TO FULLY COOPERATE AND ADJUST FOR CLERICAL
ERRORS, ANY OR ALL LOAN CLOSING DOCUMENTATION DEEMED NECESSARY OF DESIRABLE IN
THE REASONABLE DISCRETION OF LENDER TO ENABLE LENDER TO SELL, CONVEY, SEEK
GUARANTY OR MARKET SAID LOAN TO ANY ENTITY INCLUDING BUT NOT LIMITED TO AN
INVESTOR, FEDERAL NATIONAL MORTGAGE AUTHORITY OR THE VETERANS ADMINISTRATION.

THE UNDERSIGNED BORROWER(S) DO HEREBY SO AGREE AND COVENANT IN ORDER TO ASSURE
THAT THIS LOAN DOCUMENTATION EXECUTED THIS DATE WILL CONFORM AND BE ACCEPTABLE
IN THE MARKET PLACE IN THE INSTANCE OF TRANSFER, SALE OR CONVEYANCE BY LENDER
OF ITS INTEREST IN AND TO SAID LOAN DOCUMENTATION.

DATE EFFECTIVE THIS _____, 1990.

_____   _____
         WITNESS

_____   _____
         WITNESS

Sample Notice of Right to Cancel

Loan Number

NOTICE OF RIGHT TO CANCEL
Your Right to Cancel

You are entering into a transaction that will result in a mortgage on your home. You have a legal right under federal law to cancel this transaction, without cost, within three business days from whichever of the following events occurs last:

(1) The date of the transaction, which is JUNE 11, 1991; or

(2) The date you received your Truth-in-Lending disclosures; or

(3) The date you received this notice of your right to cancel.

If you cancel the transaction, the mortgage is also cancelled. Within 20 calendar days after we receive your notice, we must take the steps necessary to reflect the fact that the mortgage on your home has been cancelled, and we must return to you any money or property you have given to us or to anyone else in connection with this transaction.

You may keep any money or property we have given you until we have done the things mentioned above, but you must then offer to return the money or property. If it is impractical or unfair for you to return the property, you must offer its reasonable value. You may offer to return the property at your home or at the location of the property. The money must be returned to the address below. If we do not take possession of the money or property within 20 calendar days of your offer, you may keep it without further obligation.

How to Cancel

If you decide to cancel this transaction, you may do so by notifying us in writing, at
Yourbank, Anywhere, USA

You may use any written statement that is signed and dated by you and states your intention to cancel, or you may use this notice by dating and signing below. Keep one copy of this Notice because it contains important information about your rights.

If you cancel by mail or telegram, you must send the notice no later than midnight of JUNE 14, 1991 (or midnight of the third business day following the latest of the three events listed above). If you send or deliver your written notice to cancel some other way, it must be delivered to the above address no later than that time.

I WISH TO CANCEL

_____   _____
Consumer's Signature   Date

ACKNOWLEDGMENT OF RECEIPT

Receipt is acknowledged of the above Notice, by each of the undersigned who have received two copies of the Notice, as well as one copy of the Truth-In-Lending Disclosure Statement. Undersigned warrant that they own and reside in the principal dwelling securing this obligation, this .... day of ...., 19......

_____(SEAL)   _____(SEAL)

_____(SEAL)   _____(SEAL)

_____
(Witness)

Note: Each Resident Property Owner(s) Must Sign Above and Receive Two Copies of Notice.

CERTIFICATE OF CONFIRMATION

More than 3 business days have elapsed since the undersigned received the NOTICE OF RIGHT TO CANCEL and other Truth-in-Lending Disclosures concerning the transaction. In order to induce you to proceed with disbursement of the loan proceeds, the undersigned warrant, covenant and certify that the persons entitled to rescind the transaction have not exercised their right to rescind; that they do not wish to and will not rescind the transaction; and that they ratify and confirm the transaction in all respects. They further represent that the undersigned are the only persons entitled to rescind, because they own and reside in the principal dwelling securing the rescindable transaction; this .... day of ...., 19......

_____(SEAL)   _____(SEAL)

_____(SEAL)   _____(SEAL)

_____
(Witness)

NOTE: All parties who execute Acknowledgment of Receipt must execute Certificate of Confirmation.

Chapter 7
Credit Cards and Other Open-End Consumer Credit Loans

What is Open-End Credit?

An open end credit plan is one under which the creditor reasonably expects repeated transactions, which prescribes the terms of the transactions, and which provides for a finance charge which may be computed from time to time on the outstanding unpaid balance. A credit card account and a credit line are examples of open end credit plans.

Information That Must be Disclosed

Before opening any account under an open-end consumer credit plan, the creditor must disclose to you each of the following items, to the extent they apply to your situation:

1. The conditions under which a finance charge may be imposed, including the time period (if any) within which any credit extended may be repaid without incurring a finance charge; except that the creditor may, at his election and without disclosure, impose no finance charge if payment is received after the termination of the time period. If no time period is provided for repayment, the creditor must disclose this fact.
2. The method of determining the balance upon which a finance charge will be imposed.
3. The method of determining the amount of the finance charge, including any minimum or fixed amount imposed as a finance charge.

4. Where one or more periodic rates (different rates in different time periods) may be used to compute the finance charge, each such rate, the range of balances to which it applies, and the corresponding nominal annual percentage rate determined by multiplying the periodic rate by the number of periods in a year.

5. Identification of other charges which may be imposed as part of the plan, and their method of computation.

6. In cases where the credit is or will be secured, a statement that a security interest has been or will be taken in (a) the property purchased as part of the credit transaction, or (b) property not purchased as part of the credit transaction identified by item or type.

> **Example:** Before opening an account under an open-end credit plan, the seller said only that it might, at its option, retain a security interest in merchandise at the time the purchaser bought merchandise. The seller failed to specifically disclose the conditions under which it would retain or acquire any security interest. The failure to disclose was a violation of this section. (Under federal law, a creditor is not allowed to take the following items as collateral unless the loan is being made for the purchase of the items: clothing, furniture, appliances, linens, china, kitchenware, television, wedding rings, and other personal effects.)

7. A statement of the protection provided as to the creditor's and your responsibilities. With respect to one billing cycle per calendar year, at intervals of not less than six months or more than eighteen months, the creditor must send a statement to each borrower to whom the creditor is required to send a statement which contains the information as described below.

Since the purpose of this law is to permit informed credit shopping, the required disclosures should be made *before* a credit transaction is completed.

Billing Disclosure Requirements

After the credit is extended, your creditor will send you statements. In each billing cycle your creditor is required to send you certain information, including:

1. The outstanding balance in the account at the beginning of the statement period;

2. The amount, date, and a brief description of each extension of credit during the billing period;
3. The total amount credited to the account during the period;
4. The amount of any finance charge added to the bill during the period;
5. If more than one rate is used (for example, a cash advance often accrues a different interest rate from credit card purchases), the breakdown of the charges;
6. The total finance charge billed as an annual percentage rate;
7. The balance on which the finance charge was computed and a statement of how the balance was determined;
8. The outstanding balance in the account at the end of the period;
9. The date by which payment must be made to avoid additional finance charges;
10. The address to which you are to make inquiries about your billing.

Penalties for Violations

The penalties for violating any of the above requirements are (these are the same as those for failure to comply with disclosure requirements for credit as listed in Chapter 6):
1. any actual damage sustained by the borrower as a result of the failure;
2. twice the amount of any finance charge in connection with the transaction;
3. the reasonable attorneys fees and costs incurred in a successful legal action.

Consumer Loan Billing Procedures

Billing for consumer loan payments is regulated by the Fair Credit Billing Act (Public Law 93-495). If a bill is incorrect, you should notify the creditor, in writing, within 60 days after the creditor sent you the bill. The notice to the creditor should state your name and account number, that you believe the bill to be incorrect, and your reasons why. (See page 76.) Unless the creditor then hears from you otherwise, the creditor has 30 days after receiving your letter of dispute to send you written acknowledgment of your dispute, and then within two billing cycles after that (no more than 90 days), must make appropriate corrections on your bill and notify you of the corrections, or must make an investigation.

If the creditor's investigation shows that the amount is correct, then the creditor must send you a written explanation, along with any supporting documents. If you have disputed the bill based upon the fact you have been charged for goods never delivered to you, then the creditor should delete the charge unless it is determined that the goods were actually delivered, mailed or otherwise sent to you. The creditor must have a statement showing that fact.

A creditor who does not follow the rules under this law forfeits any right to collect from you the amount you have disputed and any finance charge on that amount (total not to exceed $50.00).

After the creditor has received notice from you under this Act, the creditor may not threaten to report adversely to anyone about your credit standing because of your failure to pay the disputed amount.

Unsolicited Credit Cards

The law provides that "no credit card shall be issued except in response to a request or application therefor." (This does not apply to renewal of, or substitution for, a credit card which you previously accepted.) If you receive a credit card for which you have not applied, the issuing company is fully responsible for its use. However, if you sign the card, use it or notify the company that you will keep it, then in many states you have "accepted" the card and will be liable for charges.

When a Credit Card is Lost or Stolen

As the holder of a credit card, you will be liable for the unauthorized use of that card only if:
1.   The card is an accepted credit card;
2.   The liability is not in excess of $50.00;
3.   The card issuer gives adequate notice to you of your potential liability;
4.   The card issuer has given you a description of how to notify the card issuer of a loss or theft (this can be printed on the billing statement);
5.   The unauthorized use is before the card issuer has been notified that an unauthorized use has occurred or may occur as a result of loss or theft; and
6.   The card issuer has provided a method whereby you can be identified as the person authorized to use the card.

In order to hold you liable, the card issuer must prove that the use was authorized, or that there are valid reasons for holding you liable. However, if you allow someone else to use your card, even if you limit the amount charged and the limit is exceeded, this is not considered unauthorized use.

For Further Research

The laws regarding open end consumer credit plans are found in Title 15, United States Code, Chapter 41, Subchapter I, Sections 1637 through 1666(j); correction of billing errors is explained in Section 1666. Sample forms as prescribed by the Federal Trade Commission are found in Title 15, United Stated Code Annotated, 12 Code of Federal Regulations, Appendix G.

Sample Letter

September 23, 1996

VISA   CERTIFIED MAIL
213 Interest Street   RETURN RECEIPT REQUESTED
Sometown, Anystate   P-396-388-492

     RE: Account No. 5555-5555-5555-5555
            Name   Jane Doe

Dear Sir or Madam:

This letter is to notify you of an error in my March
statement. The amount shown on the statement as
being charged for prescriptions from Jake's
Pharmacy is $114.00. The total cost of the
prescriptions was actually $14.00.

According to the Credit Billing Act, you have 30
days to confirm that you have received this letter
unless you correct the item before that time. You
then have two billing cycles in which to investigate
and either confirm the $114.00 amount or correct
the billing.

Enclosed is a copy of my bill from Jake's Pharmacy.
Thank you.

                            Sincerely,

                            Jane Doe
                            1423 Egypt Lane
                            Denver, CO 80034

Chapter 8
Consumer Lease Disclosures

The Consumer Leasing Act of 1976 (Public Law 94-240) regulates the types of disclosures which must be made in a consumer lease.

What is a Consumer Lease?

A consumer lease, as defined in the Act, is a contract for the use of personal property for more than four months, and for a total payment of no more than $25,000.00, primarily for personal, family or household purposes. Most commonly leased items are automobiles and furniture, however, any property which is not real estate is included in the regulations. The "lessee" is the person who is offered a lease; the "lessor" is the person offering to lease or arranging to lease under a consumer lease. It makes no difference that the lessee has the option to purchase the property at the end of the lease term.

Disclosure Requirements

Before the lease transaction is completed, the lessor must provide you with certain information, set out clearly and accurately. This information includes:
1. A brief description of the leased property;
2. The amount of any payment required at the time the lease term begins;

3. The amount payable by you for any fees, registration, certificate of title, or license fees or taxes;

4. The amount of other charges payable by you which are not included in the periodic payments, a description of the charges and that you will be liable for the difference, if any, between the anticipated fair market value of the leased property and its appraised actual value at the termination of the lease, if the lease includes such liability;

5. A statement of the amount or method of determining the amount of any liabilities the lease imposes upon you at the end of the term and whether or not you have the option to purchase the leased property and at what price and time;

6. A statement setting forth all express warranties and guarantees made by the manufacturer or lessor with respect to the leased property; and identifying the party responsible for maintaining or servicing the leased property together with a description of the responsibility;

7. A description of the insurance paid for by you, or the insurance required of you, including the types and amounts of coverages and costs;

8. A description of any security interest held or to be retained by the lessor in connection with the lease and a clear identification of the property to which the security interest relates;

9. The number, amount, and due date or periods of payments under the lease and the total amount of such periodic payments;

10. If the lease provides that you will be responsible for paying the anticipated fair market value of the property on expiration of the lease, the lessor must disclose the fair market value of the property at the beginning of the lease, the total cost of the lease at the time is terminates, and the difference between the two amounts;

11. A statement of the terms under which you can terminate the lease before the end of the lease term and the method of determining any penalty or other charge for delinquency, default, late payments, or early termination.

The disclosures can be made in the lease contract to be signed by you, and, where the lessor may be unable to provide exact dollar amounts, estimates can be given.

An advertisement by a radio broadcast to aid, promote or assist in consumer leasing must meet the above disclosure advertisements, state the number, amounts, due dates or periods of scheduled payments and the total payments, and must provide a toll-free number for consumers to use. The telephone number must be available for at least ten days from the date of the broadcast.

Residual Value Calculation

The "residual value" is the value of the property after you've made all of the lease payments. If your lease includes an estimated residual value of the property, the estimate must be a reasonable approximation of the anticipated actual fair market value of the property at the expiration of the lease. The estimated residual value may be considered unreasonable if it exceeds the actual residual value by more than three times a single monthly lease payment. (This does not take into consideration a situation where the property is damaged beyond reasonable wear and tear—the lessor may set standards for reasonable wear and tear.) If the estimated residual value is greater than three times the actual residual value, this may also be considered as evidence that the lessor acted in bad faith, and in that case the lessor cannot collect the excess amount unless a court grants a judgment in favor of the lessor. Of course, you can make a final adjustment with the lessor regarding the excess residual after the termination of the lease.

If a lease has a residual value provision at the termination of the lease, you may, at your own expense, get a professional appraisal of the property by an independent third party agreeable to both the lessor and to you. The appraisal will then be binding on both parties.

Penalties or Other Charges

Any penalties or other charges provided for in the lease must be reasonable in light of the actual harm caused to the lessor.

Liabilities of Lessor for Violations

If a lessor has violated any of the requirements under the Consumer Leasing Act, the lessor may be subject to the following liabilities as under other disclosure requirements:
1. any actual damage sustained by you as a result of the violation;
2. 25% per cent of the total amount of monthly payments under the lease, except that the liability under this provision will not be less than $100 or greater than $1,000.00;
3. your reasonable attorneys fees and costs incurred if your legal action is successful.

In a successful court action by a lessee, the lessor is required to pay the lessee's attorneys fees. For violations under the Consumer Leasing Act, a court action must be brought within one year of the termination of the lease agreement.

For Further Research

The Federal laws regarding consumer leases are found in Title 15, United States Code, Subchapter I, Part E, Sections 1667 through 1667(e). The regulations are found in Title 12 of the Code of Federal Regulations, Part 226, Truth in Lending, Section 226.15.

Title 15, United States Code, Section 1667 (c) addresses the liability of advertisers of consumer leases.

Chapter 9
Real Estate Loan Foreclosures

Mortgages

A mortgage is a lien the bank or other lender has against your real property, or an interest your lender has in your real property, as security for the note you've signed to pay for the property. (Real property refers to real estate; personal property usually refers to any other type of property.) Your mortgage is probably your largest debt, and you may need to make formal arrangements to delay payment. The most common form is the institutional mortgage (including VA and FHA) given by banks and savings and loans. If you've taken out an "equity line" against your home or other real estate, you probably have a second mortgage against the property. (The "equity line" is a line of credit given by a lender using the equity you have in your real property as collateral.) If the seller loaned you money to buy the property, he probably has a "purchase money mortgage."

A second mortgage is a loan for which some additional value in the real property was given as collateral after the original, or primary, mortgage. In order to help you buy the property, the seller may have given you a second or even a third mortgage. In many cases these are interest only, or amortized over a long period of time with a balloon payment due in five years or so. Also, if a lender loans you money to make improvements to the property (or for other purposes previously explained in Chapter 6), the lender may have taken out a second or third mortgage on your property. Any other lender who holds a mortgage on your property, or anyone who has a lien against your property either by virtue of a judgment or otherwise (as explained in Chapter 1) besides the first mortgage holder, can foreclose its mortgage. However, when title to the property is transferred at the foreclosure sale, whoever buys will take the property subject to the first or prior mortgages.

The important point to remember is this—if you have several mortgages against your property, keeping the first one current is not enough. If you don't keep the other(s) current, a foreclosure action may still be filed by the other mortgage holder(s), which would then foreclose their interest in your property subject to the first or prior mortgage(s). They may then pay off the first or prior mortgage(s).

A mortgage can be foreclosed only through court action.

Contract or Agreement for Deed

In some states the "Contract for Deed," "Agreement for Deed," or "Land Contract" is still used, where title to the property does not actually transfer to the buyer until a certain specified amount of money is paid toward the purchase. Although your seller may have led you to believe that, if you don't pay, he may immediately reclaim the property and require you to leave, you should confirm that fact with an attorney.

In many states the seller must go through formal foreclosure proceedings just as if title had transferred when the sale was made. The law often provides a purchaser under a Contract or Agreement for Deed with "equitable title" to the property and will protect that interest as it does the interest of an actual legal title holder. To protect your interest as purchaser of the property, you should determine whether the Contract or Agreement for Deed can be recorded in your local public records. This will put others on notice of your interest in the property.

If your seller under a Contract for Deed has required you to sign a "quit claim deed" at the time you signed the Contract for Deed, allowing your seller to record the transfer of title back to him/her if you fail to make the payments as required, you should check the law in your state to determine whether this is legal. In some states such a deed or transfer of title back to the seller at the time you signed the Contract or Agreement for Deed would be void (or voidable).

Deed of Trust

Many states use the Deed of Trust as the form of indebtedness to the lender. This involves three parties—the beneficiary, or lender, the trustor, or borrower, and the trustee, an independent third party which holds the trust deed. The trust deed is the document signed over by you, the borrower, to the trustee, which gives the trustee the power to sell your property if you fail to make the payments required on the note you signed promising to make payments to the lender.

Read Your Loan Documents

Your note and mortgage, trust deed, or other loan documents should spell out the terms of your loan, including the total amount of the mortgage and the monthly payments. You may also have a grace period—a specified number of days in which to make the payment—before late payment charges or additional interest can be added. Review all the documents carefully and, if you don't understand them, call your lender and ask. Most mortgages must meet the Truth in Lending requirements explained in Chapter 6.

The Mortgage Foreclosure Process

Although the procedural details may vary from state to state, a mortgage foreclosure generally works like this: Your lender will notify you that your payment is late, and that it must be brought current. If that particular payment and subsequent payments are not made, the lender then, usually through an attorney at this point, notifies you that if you do not pay the required amount, the lender will begin foreclosure proceedings.

A lawsuit is then filed, advising the court that no payments have been received for the specified time period, that the lender is exercising its right to "accelerate" the mortgage, and that the lender is entitled to foreclose its mortgage. In other words, the lender is asking that the property be taken from you by court order and sold to the highest bidder, and that any interest you may have be "foreclosed."

After the lawsuit is filed, you will be either served with a summons or notice of the foreclosure will be published in the local paper which publishes legal notices, and there is a period of time in which responses must be filed. If you don't file any written defenses with the court, which happens often, the case is set for hearing. The judge will then order that the mortgage be foreclosed and that a date for sale be set. Notice of the sale is published, and the property is sold to the highest bidder.

Service of Process and Deficiency Judgments

If the lender or mortgage holder (plaintiff) makes a diligent effort and is still unable to find you in order to have you personally served with the summons from the court, in most cases notice of the foreclosure lawsuit can be published in a local newspaper. If you are served only by publication—in other words, you are not personally served with a summons—then the lender can take the property and no more. However, if you are *properly* served, and the property does not sell at the foreclosure sale for the amount awarded in the court's judgment of foreclosure, you may be held personally liable for any "deficiency." A deficiency is the difference between the amount of the judgment and the lesser amount of the actual sale price. For example, if the judgment was for $100,000 and the property sold for only $90,000, there is a $10,000 deficiency. Again, this will depend upon the terms of your particular note and mortgage.

A deficiency judgment is like any other judgment and the same options are available to the creditor (the former mortgage holder) for collection. In some states the deficiency judgment is entered automatically; in others, the creditor must go to the court after the sale and ask that judgment be entered. California does not allow a first mortgage holder to get a deficiency judgment; a few other states restrict the availability of a deficiency judgment.

You can argue to the court that the lender should not be granted a deficiency judgment against you if the sale price for the property at the foreclosure sale was unreasonably low. The court has the right to look into the relationship between the lender and the buyer of your property and decide whether there was any misconduct or collusion, in which case a judge can refuse to enter a deficiency judgment. If the value of the property exceeds the debt, the judge can refuse to give the lender a deficiency judgment against you. At this stage of the proceeding you need to present as much evidence as possible to the court, including an appraisal of the property's fair market value, which might cause a judge to decide in your favor. If you can afford it, you may want to have an appraisal of the property done on the date of sale.

If the property sells at the foreclosure sale for an amount higher than the amount of the judgment plus any added-on legal interest, then you may be entitled to the excess amount.

After the Sale — Period of Redemption

Most states have a "period of redemption" after the sale takes place wherein the owner can pay the amount of the judgment to the court, plus any legal interest, and redeem his property. This time period is set by law, and varies from state to state (for example, the "period of redemption" is ten days in Florida, six months in Kansas). As another possible solution to the foreclosure, you may be able to transfer this right to redeem your property to someone else, who can then in turn either lease or sell the property back to you.

Foreclosing a Deed of Trust

A trust deed is advantageous to the lender because the lender does not have to go to court to foreclose its loan. If you do not meet your obligations under the note, a notice of default can be recorded in your local county records. *Once it is recorded and you've received a copy, the foreclosure process has begun.* Most states give you a certain period of time after the notice is recorded and you've received your copy in which you can reinstate the loan. In order to reinstate the loan, you must bring the payments current, and pay any interest and penalties.

After the period allowed for reinstatement has run, the trustee must advertise the property for sale for a minimum period of time. You will find the advertisement in a paper containing legal notices—probably not in your regular newspaper. After the time for advertising has run, the property is sold to the highest bidder. Often the lender (in this case the "beneficiary") is the highest bidder. Following the sale, your state may give you an additional period of time to "redeem" the property.

What if You Sell the Property Before Foreclosure?

If you sell the property before the lender forecloses, your buyer, the title insurance company or attorney handling the closing will research the title and find that the property has a mortgage or deed of trust (or mortgages or liens) against it. If your buyer takes title to the property in spite of the mortgage (instead of paying off the mortgage and getting a mortgage release or satisfaction), and assumes and agrees with you that he will make the mortgage payments to you or directly to the lender, your obligation to make the payments has not automatically been eliminated.

Many mortgages and notes contain a "due on sale clause." In other words, if there is a transfer of title without the lender's approval, the lender may declare the entire balance of the mortgage due and payable in full. Although beyond the scope of this book, you should carefully review your loan documents before considering such a transfer. Even if there is no due-on-sale clause, you will not be relieved of the debt. Many bank loans require that a new buyer qualify and pay a certain amount to the bank before the bank will relieve you and accept the new owner as the borrower.

If you do not get a release from your lender, the lender can proceed with foreclosure if your buyer does not make the payments as he promised you he would. Not only will your buyer be named as a defendant in the foreclosure lawsuit, but you will also be named as a defendant as the person obligated on note and mortgage. The lender may still get a deficiency judgment against you.

Example: Beverly and Jim bought a home in Florida from John. John gave Beverly and Jim a deed to the property, and Beverly and Jim in turn gave John a note and mortgage. John financed 80 per cent of the purchase price of the property. Beverly and Jim then sold the property to Charles, and Charles agreed to make the payments to John. When Charles failed to continue making payments, John filed a lawsuit to foreclose his mortgage on the property. Beverly and Jim, although they had sold the property to Charles, were named as defendants in the lawsuit. John had no agreement with Charles, only with Beverly and Jim. The property was purchased at the foreclosure sale for less than the amount of money owed on the mortgage plus attorneys fees and court costs. John asked the court to enter a deficiency judgment against Beverly and Jim for the difference.

Deed in Lieu of Foreclosure

If you find yourself in a position where you are simply unable to continue making your payments and cannot sell your property, you may want to suggest to your lender that it take a "deed in lieu of foreclosure." This is a deed transferring title of the property to the lender, in exchange for the lender's agreement to forego the foreclosure proceeding and forego obtaining a deficiency judgment against you (in a state which allows deficiency judgments in mortgage foreclosures). In your negotiations, you should also ask that the lender allow you to live in the property for a certain period of time after the transfer of title.

Not all lenders will accept this as an alternative, especially if you have other assets and the lender believes it can collect a deficiency judgment. Most lenders would prefer not to own real estate, particularly where the value of the property is less than the amount of the mortgage. However, this is an alternative which you may wish to consider.

A deed in lieu of foreclosure may be a good alternative if the mortgage holder is the person from whom you bought the property. The seller would then have the property back to sell again, and he will also have had the benefit of the downpayment you paid when you bought the property.

Since this is recorded in your local public records, a credit reporting agency may report the deed in lieu of foreclosure on your credit report.

Negotiating With Your Lender and FHA Extensions

Your lender may also be willing to work with you during economic hardships, and take partial payments for a period of time or forego payments until you are able to resume the regular payment schedule. (Particularly in bad economic times, lenders usually do not want to own your real estate—they want the money. Even if they get the property back through foreclosure, they probably won't be able to get the money.) You and the lender are, in most cases, looking for the same thing—a way in which the bank can minimize its losses and you can keep the property. As a result of the large number of delinquencies in home loans, some lenders have even established departments for the specific purpose of working out loan payment problems with borrowers.

When you realize you're having financial difficulties, set an appointment with the bank's loan department manager, or have a personal meeting with the officer who is in charge of your loan. You should begin with a positive attitude—that you are willing to work out your financial problem *with* the lender. Explain your circumstances, and that you are committed to meeting your obligations. Empathize with the lender's position in a tough financial market. If the officer is not responding favorably to your appeal, you should point out that you may consider bankruptcy as an option. This would tie up the property for a considerable length of time, and cost the lender both interest and legal fees. (If you file bankruptcy, the lender probably won't be able to get a deficiency judgment against you.) The officer may well decide it is much better to negotiate with you than to take such a loss.

An individual or private lender may be willing to work with you through your difficult times, particularly if you had previously been prompt in making your payments. In negotiating with a private lender, you should find out what the lender does or intends to do with the loan payment. Perhaps he will extend your loan in exchange for an increase in the interest rate. It is important to consider a number of different alternatives.

If you have an FHA (Federal Housing Administration) loan on your house, you may be able to work out an extension of your payments. The FHA insures the loans that institutional lenders make to you. If you default on your FHA loan, the lender may turn the property over to FHA and collect its money. In order to help you stay out of foreclosure, the FHA has a plan which may help you.

If you are behind three months or more on your payments, your lender will send you a letter regarding your default and a form for you to complete explaining your financial situation. After receiving your completed form, the lender can then transfer your loan to HUD (Department of Housing and Urban Development), or you may contact your local HUD office directly and explain that you have an FHA insured mortgage and that you are unable to make the payments due to circumstances beyond your control, usually an illness or job lay-off. (The property must be your primary residence and your only FHA property.) You must also be able to show that you will be able to begin making payments again within a certain time period. If you meet the requirements, a plan will be worked out whereby you will have a certain time period in which to bring the payments current.

More detailed information on this program is available through your local HUD office.

If you have a balloon payment (the term usually refers to a payment which is more than twice larger than any other payment under the loan) coming due which you are unable to make, try to get your lender to refinance the loan. You may be able to make larger payments over a period of time and pay off the balance due. With some creative thought and a clear idea of what your lender's objectives are, you may be able to come up with some alternatives to pay the balance due.

All possibilities should be explored before you allow the foreclosure process to go forward, find yourself served with a summons and then possibly have a deficiency judgment entered against you. Remember, both the foreclosure action and the judgment will be shown on your credit report and may negatively affect your ability to get credit in the future.

If You Are in the Military

The Soldiers' and Sailors' Civil Relief Act may just apply to you. A lender cannot foreclose out of court (on a deed of trust) if you are in the military service. The plaintiff in a court foreclosure action must file a sworn statement with the court stating whether or not you are in the military service. If the plaintiff states that either (1) he doesn't know, or (2) you are in the military service, the court cannot enter a judgment against you until an attorney has been appointed to represent you and the attorney is heard on your behalf.

Recap — Steps You Can Take After Foreclosure is Started

Recently the news media has presented numerous stories about foreclosures, particularly in those areas of the country hardest hit economically. Your best approach is to negotiate with your lender *before* the foreclosure process is started and reach an agreement to extend, refinance, or otherwise work out your problem. In some cases, of course, there is not much you can do to prevent the inevitable. Once the foreclosure process has begun, you can still stop or at least delay the process by:

- reaching an agreement with the lender which will reduce your payment for a period of time ("forbearance agreement"). The lender may accept whatever you are able to pay, and accrue the balance owed over time to be added onto the mortgage, or give you an extension, turning the missed payments into a debt payable during or after the original term of the loan.
- if there is a second (or third, etc.) loan against your property, perhaps you can negotiate with that lender to pay off the first and incorporate the amount into the second, resulting in only one loan for you to pay.
- reading your loan papers carefully to determine whether you have the right to bring the payments current after foreclosure is filed. (Remember that if the loan is in the form of a trust deed, you should be able to bring the payments current before the notice of sale is published). If so, you may be able to raise the funds to reinstate the loan—i.e., arrange a loan from a friend, refinance through the same or another lender, take in a co-owner or partner who perhaps will help you bring the loan current in exchange for a portion of the equity in the property, etc. You may even have a family member who is willing to co-sign or give you a loan to help you through your crisis.
- in a mortgage foreclosure, filing your written response to the foreclosure action with the court. The court will then allow both you and the lender to present your cases. In your written response, you should dispute any inaccuracies in your lender's figures, inaccuracies in the legal description or other lender errors, and present as a counterclaim against the foreclosure complaint any claim you have against the lender for violation of the Truth in Lending disclosure requirements (see Chapter 6).
- in a mortgage foreclosure action, telling the court that service was improper. Even after the sale, in some instances you may be able to have the entire foreclosure set aside (made null and void) by the court if you can show that you were available to be served by the lender, yet instead of personally serving you with a summons, notice was published in the newspaper.
- challenging the trust deed documents in court. By proving to the court that the documents do not include information required by law, the entire foreclosure process can be made null and void. Regulation Z requirements must be met in most situations (see Chapter 6).
- getting your lender to agree to accept a deed in lieu of foreclosure, if you have no defense and you can avoid a deficiency judgment
- using the threat of (or filing) bankruptcy
- if the lender has threatened you or attempted to intimidate you, you may have the basis for a lawsuit against the lender. (You

should set these facts out in your written defense to the foreclosure.)

(The Federal Trade Commission has the authority to protect you
from a lender's unfair and deceptive practices used in foreclosure.)

At the end of this Chapter is a sample notice of sale under a Deed
in Trust. There is also a mortgage foreclosure complaint and a sample
response ("Answer"). In your response to a court action, you should
first answer each statement made by the lender in the complaint. Then,
if you agree that some of the statements made by the lender in the
complaint are correct, but you have further explanations or reasons
which you believe the court should be made aware of, these should be
set out in your Answer as "Affirmative Defenses." If you have any
claim against the lender— for example, violation of a disclosure requirement under Regulation Z— this should be stated in a "Counterclaim" or "Countersuit" along with your answer to the lender's charges.

It is possible to have a foreclosure judgment set aside (withdrawn)
even after the redemption period has passed if you can show to the
court that the lender did not make a sufficient effort to find and notify
you, or that some other error occurred in the foreclosure action. Finally,
borrowers are fighting back against lenders who were once aggres-
sively competing for the borrowers' business. Lawsuits range from a 1.5
billion dollar claim based on fraud and conspiracy in forcing a silver
and oil business into bankruptcy, to damages caused by a lender's
delays in processing loans. If you think you may have the basis for a
lawsuit against your lender, you should get the advice of an attorney.

For Further Research

To determine whether your state uses Deeds of Trust or Mortgages,
simply look at your loan documents. Then obtain information from
your lender regarding Regulation Z and contact your regional Federal
Trade Commission Office for further literature. If your mortgage might
be foreclosed, read your state's statutes regarding the legal procedure
for filing a foreclosure action, noting the maximum time periods
allowed for the various steps in the process. Note how long you have
to redeem your property after the sale. When you research your state's
statutes, ask the librarian for an "annotated" version. This will include
cases which might help clarify certain provisions of the law. The cases
will also give you an idea of what kinds of defenses other people in
situations similar to yours have presented to the court.

Your local law library might have how-to books on mortgage
foreclosure defenses such as those published by your state bar associa-

tion continuing legal education committee. HUD publishes a pamphlet "Avoiding Mortgage Default" available at your local HUD office or your mortgage lender's office.

The applicable provision of the Soldiers' and Sailors' Civil Relief Act is found in the United States Code Appendix 50, Section 532 (50 Ap Sec. 532).

Responding to a Foreclosure Complaint

A complaint for foreclosure will usually contain numbered paragraphs, stating why the mortgage is entitled to foreclose. You will need to respond to each statement in the complaint, by either admitting or denying them.

The sample answer on the following page is based on a complaint which contains the following numbered paragraphs alleging that:

---

1. This is an action to foreclose a mortgage on real property located in Lee County, Florida, and for damages in excess of $5,000.00.

2. On or about June 9, 1996, the defendants executed and delivered a note to the plaintiff secured by a mortgage on the real property that is the subject of this action. Copies of the note and mortgage are attached hereto as Exhibits "A" and "B," respectively, and the terms thereof are incorporated herein by reference. The real property that is the subject of this action is described in the mortgage.

3. The defendants failed to pay the installment under the note due, despite demand therefor by the plaintiff.

4. There is now due and owing under the note the principal sum of $39,278.24, together with accrued interest to March 1, 1990 in the amount of $262.50, plus per diem thereafter at the rate of $8.63.

5. The lien represented by the mortgage is superior to the estate or interest of the defendants and anyone claiming by, through or under the defendants.

6. That the property which is the subject of this action is residential rental property, and that a receiver should be appointed by the court to insure the continued maintenance and care of the subject property.

7. The plaintiff has retained the services of the undersigned law firm and has agreed to pay said firm a reasonable fee for the prosecution of this action.

8. All conditions precedent to the institution of this action have occurred, been performed or excused.

Sample Answer to Foreclosure Complaint

IN THE CIRCUIT COURT OF THE NINTH JUDICIAL
CIRCUIT IN AND FOR LEE COUNTY, FLORIDA

XYZ Mortgage Corp. _____)
         Plaintiff,   )
)
vs.   )   Case No. __96-0734____
)
John Doe and Jane Doe)
        Defendants.)

ANSWER

COME NOW the Defendants, ___John Doe and___
___Jane Doe___, and for their answer to Plaintiff's
Complaint, state as follows:

1. Paragraphs 1 and 2 are admitted.
2. Paragraphs 3 and 4 are denied.
3. Defendants are without knowledge to either admit or deny paragraph 5.
4. Paragraph 6 is denied.
5. Defendants are without knowledge to either admit or deny paragraph 7.
6. Paragraph 8 is denied.

WHEREFORE, defendants respectfully request that the court grant judgment in their favor, and for such other and further relief as the court deems proper.

AFFIRMATIVE DEFENSES

11. The amount currently due under the Note and Mortgage is $72,695.98, not the amount the plaintiff claims is due.
12. Defendants offered plaintiff the amount due on July 23, 1996, but plaintiff refused to accept payment.

WHEREFORE, defendants respectfully request that judgment be granted in their favor, and for such other relief as the Court deems proper.

COUNTERCLAIM

1. Plaintiff failed to provide defendants with the correct financial disclosures as required under the Federal Truth in Lending Act, specifically set forth as follows: Plaintiff failed to properly calculate and inform Defendants of the annual percentage rate of interest.

2. As a result of such failure to provide defendants with the correct financial disclosures, defendants have suffered damages in the amount of approximately $10,000 as follows: Excess interest paid in the amount of $7,248.73, plus additional damages to be proven at trial.

3. Plaintiff has threatened defendants for non-payment by threatening to contact defendants' employers and neighbors.

WHEREFORE, defendants pray that judgment be granted in their favor in the amount of $10,000.00, and for such other relief as the Court deems proper.

Dated: September 12, 1996.

_____

_____

John Doe & Jane Doe, Defendants

12 Easy St., Ft. Myers, FL 99999

Tel. (813) 555-5555

Other sample affirmative defenses (paragraph 12):
1. "defendant was not properly served with summons."
2. "the property described in plaintiff's complaint is not the property which is described in plaintiff's loan documents."
3. "defendant has been properly maintaining the property."

A copy of this Answer should be sent to the plaintiff and anyone else required by the court.

NOTE: Some states require that you explain very specifically in your complaint or answer the facts surrounding your claim; others allow you to be more general and leave the specifics to be spelled out a later date during the court proceedings.

Chapter 10
Repossession of Personal Property — Foreclosure

When you buy a car and get financing, you normally give the lender or bank a security interest (lien) in the vehicle. Your state might not require any additional notice of the security interest in property to which you hold a title other than the notice that is placed by the lender directly on the title. On other personal property without a title, the bank or financing company may file what is known as a financing statement, which serves the same purpose as a mortgage or deed of trust on real estate. The statement is recorded in the appropriate state office (usually the Secretary of State or your county). It is the lender's duty to make sure that its security interest is properly filed. The financing statement must contain the lender's and your signatures, must clearly identify the property, and must be filed in the correct place.

Just as in a sale of real estate, when you sell the property, the lien must be satisfied or the buyer takes the property subject to the lien and you will still be responsible for payment. The lender can, of course, consent to the transfer of the property and release you from your responsibility. (You may also be violating a provision of your loan agreement and subjecting yourself to criminal and civil prosecution by selling the property without paying off the lender.)

Unless you have an agreement with the lender to the contrary, if you do not pay, or if you otherwise don't live up to your agreement with the lender (such as failing to maintain the required insurance or letting the property deteriorate), the lender has the right to repossess the property as long as there is no breach of the peace. The lender may then sell it and then get a deficiency judgment against you much like the mortgage foreclosure process. For example, if you have repeatedly missed car loan payments at the bank, the bank may contract with someone to repossess the car. Your car can be picked up wherever it can be found. It is then sold, and you may be held responsible for the difference between the amount it sold for and the amount left on the loan, plus attorneys fees and court costs (the deficiency).

Whoever repossesses the property must do so without breach of the peace. In other words, if the property (furniture or appliances, for example) is located in your home, you must consent to the creditor's entry and repossession. Damage to the property by the creditor while it is being repossessed may be considered a breach of the peace.

However, if the property is accessible without entering your home or a closed building, then there is no breach of the peace. For example, if your car is parked in your driveway, the creditor may walk up, get into the car and drive it off without violating any law (provided he does not damage the vehicle). If there is damage to your property, you may have a legal case against the lender.

Restrictions on Repossession

The laws regarding secured transactions restrict what the lender can do when repossessing collateral. For example:

- A lender may *not* exert undue pressure on you to repossess an item and has no right to use force.
- A lender is liable to you for any damage caused to the property when it is repossessed.
- A lender may repossess the property without court action only if it can be done without breaching the peace.

Sale of Collateral After Repossession

After repossessing the property, the lender may sell it, lease it, or otherwise dispose of it in a "commercially reasonable" manner. The property may be sold in its condition at the time of repossession or after reasonable preparation for sale by the creditor. "Commercially reasonable" generally means that the property must be sold in keeping with the prevailing trade and business practices.

The proceeds of the sale are applied first to the cost of repossession and selling the property, including attorney's fees and legal expenses if provided for in your agreement, next, to satisfy the outstanding debt, and third to satisfy any other junior security interest in the property if the secured party has given proper notice to your creditor.

Requirements for Sale

In order for a creditor to sell collateral, the following requirements must be met:

- The creditor should give you reasonable notice of a sale unless you have waived notice.
- The creditor can purchase your property at a private sale only if the property is sold in a recognized market with standard price quotations *and* if the sale is commercially reasonable. In determining whether a sale is commercially reasonable, the method of sale, time and place of sale, adequacy of advertising, and appropriateness of wholesale versus retail disposition should be considered.
- The creditor must not allow your property to deteriorate after repossession. To do so may be a violation of the creditor's obligations and will adversely affect the creditor's ability to get a deficiency judgment against you.

Depending upon the terms of your security agreement, you may be liable for any deficiency—the difference between the amount of the sale applied to satisfy the debt and the total amount due the creditor. Just as in a mortgage foreclosure, you can argue against the deficiency judgment if you are able to show to the court that the lender sold the property for far too little money.

The lender should also notify you of the sale of the property in order to get a deficiency judgment. For example, if you loan your car to a friend, the car is wrecked and the lender accepts the insurance proceeds and turns the car over to the insurance company without notifying you, the lender cannot get a deficiency judgment against you for the balance owed.

If you have paid at least 60 per cent of the cash price of the property, after repossession the creditor must sell the property within 90 days or you may have a lawsuit against the creditor for "conversion" (taking your property and converting it to the creditor's own use), or as set forth below under "Your Remedies."

Lender's Pattern of Accepting Late Payments

If your lender has consistently accepted late payments from you, you may have a defense on the grounds that the lender's conduct led you to believe that late payments would be accepted and that you would be allowed to catch up, and that you should have been given notice of a change in the lender's policy.

Your Remedies

Soldiers' and Sailors' Civil Relief Act

If you entered into the agreement to buy personal property, such as a refrigerator or automobile, before you entered the military, the creditor cannot repossess the property without a court order. Before allowing the property to be repossessed, the court has the option to decide what is in the best interest of both parties. For example, you might be allowed to keep the property in return for smaller payment amounts to creditor.

No Proper Financing Statement

When the lender attempts to take the collateral, you may argue that the financing statement was not properly filed, or that it failed to contain certain vital information, and that therefor the lender has no valid security interest in the property.

Your Right to Redeem the Property

Any time before the creditor has sold the property, or before your debt has been paid you may redeem (take back) the property by paying to the creditor all obligations which the property secured plus any expenses the creditor incurred in taking it and preparing for its sale, including reasonable attorney fees and costs.

Reimbursement for Loss

You may recover from the creditor any loss caused you by the creditor's failure to comply with the requirements regarding repossession and sale of the property. If the property is consumer goods, then you have a right to recover an amount not less than the credit service charge plus ten per cent of the principal amount of the debt.

For example, if the creditor repossessed your boat and allowed the physical condition and value to drastically decline while keeping it for many months, failed to follow its normal repossession procedures, continued to hold it even after it filed its lawsuit for foreclosure, then sold the boat at a price less than half of its value when repossessed, you have a claim against the creditor in that the sale was not "commercially reasonable." *First Florida National Bank at Pensacola v. Martin*, App. 1 Dist., 449 So. 2d 861 (1984).

Punitive Damages

Finally, you may be entitled to punitive damages if you can show that the creditor grossly disregarded your rights. For example, where a seller had repossessed the buyer's car without warning, seller's agent inventoried the personal property in the car and yet returned the personal property to the car contrary to normal creditor procedure, the court agreed that the seller had shown wanton disregard for the buyer's rights to his personal property and gave the buyer an award of punitive damages against the seller in the amount of $1,000. *Ford Motor Credit Co. v. Waters,* App. 273 So.2d 96, (1973).

If the Lender Already Has the Collateral

Your lender may have a "security interest" in certain of your property simply by taking possession of it. If, for example, you have given your bank stocks and bonds to hold as collateral for a note you've signed, the bank may have the right to immediately sell the stocks and bonds if you do not make the required payments. The bank will apply the proceeds from the sale to the unpaid debt, plus any costs of the sale. Unless you've made other arrangements with the lender, the balance, if any is left, should be given back to you.

The same requirements for a commercially reasonable sale of repossessed property apply to a sale of property the lender already has in its possession.

For Further Research

Your state statutes should include a section on "secured transactions," in which you will find the rights and duties of the lender and borrower set forth in detail.

In addition, your state's consumer affairs office should have information available regarding your rights.

The applicable provision of the Soldiers' and Sailors' Civil Relief Act is found in the Appendix to the United States Code, 50 Ap. 531.

Chapter 11
When the Creditor Files a Lawsuit

If you haven't been able to reach an agreement with your creditors as to how and when payment will be made, there's a good possibility that you will be sued. The goal of the creditor is to get you to pay the debt, or to take your property and sell it in order to pay the debt. Unless the lawsuit is dismissed or withdrawn from the court, a judgment will be entered, either for or against you. (You may be able to work out a "deferred" judgment with the creditor, where the lawsuit is dismissed once payments are made. This will be discussed in more detail below.)

What is a Judgment?

A judgment is a decision made by a court in a lawsuit. It becomes part of the public records which are available to anyone who takes the time to obtain the information, including credit reporting agencies. A money judgment requires you to pay a certain dollar amount.

How a Creditor Gets a Judgment

A money judgment is obtained by first filing a lawsuit in the appropriate court. A lawsuit is an action whereby the "plaintiff," the person who files the lawsuit, asks the court to make a determination that he is entitled to money from you. The "petition" or "complaint" is the document that the plaintiff files with the court, stating what he feels he is entitled to and why. In legal terminology, the plaintiff is asking the court for "relief." (Deficiency judgments are discussed in Chapters 9 and 10.) The "defendant" is the person against whom the lawsuit is filed and who the plaintiff claims owes the money. The procedures for filing a lawsuit and getting a judgment may vary somewhat from one state to another, and are governed by your state court's Rules of Civil Procedure. These rules are available in your state's statute books which you should be able to find at your nearest law library, or perhaps your local public library. Your local court clerk may also be able to answer specific questions such as the manner in which a document must be filed or the time deadline for filing.

Your creditor may file a lawsuit against you if you do not pay the monies you owe. Depending upon the dollar amount the creditor is suing for and your state's laws regulating the court system, the creditor may file on his own in "Small Claims Court," or a court in which an individual can file without an attorney up to a maximum dollar amount. This is usually the least expensive method of filing a lawsuit which can be used by the creditor.

If you have a written contract with your creditor, or if your state laws so provide, the creditor may be entitled to attorney's fees if he wins the lawsuit and the court enters a judgment against you. If this is the case, the creditor will often choose to use an attorney rather than file the lawsuit himself, even if the dollar amount is small. Most bank loan documents require that you pay the attorneys fees and costs of any action taken against you to collect the money. You should read the documents carefully to determine whether the attorneys fees are chargeable against you even if the lender is unsuccessful. If your state has a law which allows attorneys fees to be charged to you only if there is "no justiciable issue," (in other words, there is absolutely no question about your liability for the amount due), then you should by all means raise a defense.

Once the lawsuit is filed, you must be served with a summons issued by the court, along with a copy of the petition or complaint. **If you are not served with summons and a copy of the petition or complaint, a judgment for payment of money usually cannot be entered against you in the court records.** The summons and petition or complaint will in most cases be served by either a sheriff's deputy or by a special process server appointed by the court.

You will have a certain period of time after you are served in which to answer the lawsuit, or a date and time will appear on the summons at which you must appear in court. If you are unable to determine from the papers what your deadline is, call the court clerk in the courthouse where the lawsuit was filed — the clerk should be able to tell you when your answer is due.

If you do choose to answer the lawsuit yourself, you should make sure that you respond to each one of the charges set forth in the petition or complaint. Sample complaints and answers are included at the end of this chapter. If you let your deadline go by without responding or appearing as required, a "default judgment" may be entered against you. In other words, the court may grant the creditor's request and enter the judgment requiring you to pay.

After the judgment is granted by the court, it may continue to accrue interest until the date it is paid. The amount of interest varies from state to state.

Your Defenses to the Petition or Complaint

If you don't care whether a default judgment is entered against you, and you don't have a defense to any of the charges in the creditor's complaint, then you don't need to do anything. Before you decide to do nothing, however, you should consider the defenses you may have to your creditor's demand for payment. Possible defenses are:

1. The creditor has already been paid;
2. The service for which the creditor is claiming payment was not performed;
3. You are not responsible for payment of the debt (i.e., the debt was incurred by a corporation--not you personally, or by your spouse — not you);
4. You were not properly served with summons.
5. The "Statute of Limitations" has lapsed — in other words, the time allowed the creditor to file suit against you for collection of the debt has passed. The Statute of Limitations in your state are found at the end of this book in Appendix D.
6. The creditor's actions in getting your promise to pay were "unconscionable," or in other words, so outrageous and over-bearing that they would shock the average person. You are telling the court that you were so taken advantage of that you had practically no alternative but to agree to creditor's terms. In order for this defense to be effective, you should have notified the creditor immediately after you agreed to pay that you wanted to cancel your agreement and the reasons why. Your defense would be even stronger if you also refused to make any payments to the creditor and, if the creditor provided you with a service such as roof repair, you immediately requested that he discontinue the work.
7. The goods you received were defective and therefore you do not owe the money.
8. The creditor has breached its warranty, i.e., has not met the conditions it is required to meet under the warranty(ies) you

received with the goods you purchased. In addition to any written warranties you received when you purchased the goods, there may be "implied warranties" (i.e., warranties that the creditor/seller gives you just by selling you the product). For example, the goods must be fit for the purpose for which they are intended to be used.

9. If a creditor is suing you for a deficiency judgment after repossessing and selling collateral, you may defend on the basis that the sale was not in a "commercially reasonable manner." (See Chapter 10.)

10. Specifically for child support, you have lost your job and request a reduction. (See page 108.)

If you were not properly served, the case should not proceed in court. Once you become aware that a judgment has been entered against you based on improper service of summons, you should immediately notify the court clerk and ask about the procedure to have the judgment set-aside (i.e., withdrawn from the court records). This may require you to appear in court and present your argument to the judge.

After the lawsuit has been properly filed and summons properly served, there are legally prescribed methods by which the attorney or plaintiff may obtain information from you and other persons regarding the claim. Ultimately, if you don't have any legitimate defenses against the lawsuit and you have been unable to settle with your creditor, the court may enter a judgment against you.

After the judgment is granted by the court, there may also be a certain period of time which you have to appeal the judgment or ask the court to rehear your case and modify or set aside the judgment before the judgment creditor can begin efforts to collect on the judgment. If you have defenses which you didn't bring up at the trial or before the judgment was entered, now is the time to let the court know. You may also have the right to appeal your case to a higher court.

What if You Move to Another State?

A creditor can take its judgment into the state where you are currently living or where your assets are located. There is a legal procedure whereby the original judgment can become a new judgment in another state. (Check to see if your state has adopted the "Uniform Enforcement of Foreign Judgments Act.") The new state's laws regarding collection of the judgment will then apply to the judgment creditor. You should be notified either by service of a summons or by certified mail from the court clerk that the judgment is being filed, and be given an opportunity to contest the judgment before any action is taken to collect it.

Confession of Judgment

A "confession of judgment" provision in a loan document gives the creditor the right to automatically get a judgment against you if you don't pay the balance owed. Such a provision is prohibited by Federal law except in a real estate contract. If your loan document does contain such a provision, it is not enforceable by the creditor.

Possible Alternatives if the Debt is Legitimate

Reduced Lump-Sum Settlement

If the debt for which the creditor is demanding payment is legitimate and you have determined that you have no defenses, perhaps your creditor would be willing to settle the debt with you before he obtains a judgment. (As will be discussed in following Chapters, "executing" on a judgment is often more difficult than getting the judgment.)

It may be more appealing to your creditor to receive a lump sum reduced amount as payment in full, rather than go to the time and expense of obtaining a judgment and then attempting to collect the amount due under the judgment.

Deferred Judgment

If the creditor has already filed his lawsuit, and if you are unable to pay a lump sum amount as settlement in full in exchange for having the lawsuit dismissed, you might suggest to the creditor that he take a "deferred" judgment. If you pay an agreed-upon amount until the balance due is paid in full, the lawsuit should then be dismissed without a judgment ever being entered against you. However, if you fail to make the required payments, the plaintiff creditor need only properly notify the court, and the court may sign the judgment.

Mediation

As an alternative to court, you can suggest to the creditor that you take your dispute to an independent, third party who will hear both sides. This can be either an arbitrator or a mediator. An arbitrator will hear both sides and then make a decision for you just like a court would do, A mediator will talk to both sides and attempt to help them come to a mutually acceptable agreement. Some states have mediation programs available to parties in dispute.

Going to Court

If your creditor is unwilling to either settle and dismiss the lawsuit or take a deferred judgment, prepare to go to court. If you are not represented by an attorney, you should have your income and assets well documented, as well as your monthly expenses and your repayment plan. (See Chapter 12.) When the creditor recognizes that you are making the best effort possible to repay the debt, it is likely that settlement will be reached before the case is actually heard by the judge. In most cases, this will be less costly for the creditor than would monthly garnishments or other methods of collecting the judgment amount. If the case is heard by a judge, the judge may order that the creditor accept the amount of money you have offered to pay.

Effect of Judgment on Credit Report

As explained in Chapter 4, a judgment may remain on your credit record for a period of seven years, unless the law of the state in which the judgment is entered allows a longer time period. State law may also allow the creditor to periodically renew the judgment, so that it remains effective for a much longer period. With regard to your credit report, you have the options set forth in Chapter 4, and of course you should offer an explanation about the circumstances surrounding the judgment to any potential lender who will review the report in making its decision whether or not to loan you money.

For Further Research

Read your state's statutes regarding the legal procedure for filing a lawsuit, noting the maximum time periods allowed for the various steps in the process. When you research your state's statutes, ask the librarian for an "annotated" version. This will include cases which might help clarify certain provisions of the law. The cases will also give you an idea of what kinds of defenses other people in situations similar to yours have presented to the court. Your court clerk may also have information about mediation or arbitration services.

The prohibition against a "confession of judgment" clause is found in 16 CFR Sec. 444 (the Code of Federal Regulations), the section of the Federal Trade Commission regulations regarding credit practices.

Sample Answer to Complaint

IN THE CIRCUIT COURT OF THE ___SIXTH___ JUDICIAL
CIRCUIT, IN AND FOR __PINELLAS__ COUNTY, FLORIDA

EASY-AIR, INC._____)
     Plaintiff,)
vs.   ) Case No. _96-3592___
JOE DOE_____)
     Defendant.)

ANSWER

Defendant, <u>Joe Doe</u>, answers plaintiff's Complaint as follows:

1. Defendant admits paragraph 1 of the Complaint.

2. Defendant admits that he entered into a business transaction with plaintiff on May 2, 1996, but denies that he agreed to pay plaintiff.

3. Defendant admits to receiving statements and a demand letter from plaintiff, and defendant responded by sending letters to plaintiff, copies of which are attached to this Answer.

4. Defendant denies paragraphs 4 and 5.

AFFIRMATIVE DEFENSES

1. In exchange for the $2,500.00 defendant was to pay to plaintiff, plaintiff was to deliver to defendant a new air conditioning system, fully installed in the defendant's home.

2. Plaintiff has failed to deliver this item to defendant, therefore, defendant does not owe any money to plaintiff.

WHEREFORE, defendant demands judgment against plaintiff.

        _____
        Joe Doe, Defendant
        1412 Heatstroke Ln.
        Clearwater, FL 34616
        (813) 555-5555

Sample Motion

IN THE CIRCUIT COURT OF THE <u>THIRTEENTH</u> JUDICIAL
CIRCUIT IN AND FOR <u>HILLSBOROUGH</u> COUNTY, FLORIDA

IN RE:)
)
MARY SMITH   )   Case No. <u>92-3394</u>
a minor   )

<u>MOTION FOR MODIFICATION OF CHILD SUPPORT</u>

   JOHN SMITH, father of MARY SMITH, hereby requests
that the court reduce the amount of child support
required to be paid under Order dated <u>May 6, 1992,</u>
for the following reasons:
   1. I was laid-off from my job at XYZ Company on
March 15, 1996.
   2. Although I have made a diligent effort, I have
been unable to find employment at a salary
comparable to what I was making at XYZ Company.
   3. I am currently working as a gardener for ABC
Landscaping, and my salary is $6.00 per hour, which
is approximately one-half of what I was paid while
employed with XYZ Company.
   WHEREFORE, I hereby ask the court that my child
support obligation be reduced to $30.00 per week .

                        _____
                        JOHN SMITH

STATE OF <u>FLORIDA</u>)
COUNTY OF <u>HILLSBOROUGH</u>)
   On this_____ day of March, 1996, before me, the
undersigned, a Notary Public in and for the above county and
State, appeared JOHN SMITH, who is personally known to me to
be the same person who executed the above Motion, and that
he did so as his free act and deed.

                        _____
                        Notary Public

Chapter 12
Collection of Money Judgments

Actions by a Judgment Creditor

After a creditor gets a judgment against you, he becomes a "judgment creditor." Once the court enters its judgment, the judgment creditor, if he knows or believes you have or are expecting to receive assets, may attempt to collect the amount due in the judgment in a number of different ways ("execute on the judgment"). First, the judgment creditor must determine what your assets are.

Judgment Creditor's Investigation

If the creditor is unsure of what your income and assets are, he may obtain this information by taking your deposition or asking you to answer interrogatories (written questions). Other forms of investigation include checking whether you have a vehicle registered in your name and checking with the property appraiser to find out what, if any, real property you own. If you gave your judgment creditor a financial statement when you obtained the loan, the creditor will also review the statement again to see what assets you represented to him that you own.

In a deposition (or by written interrogatories), the creditor may ask you questions such as:
1. If you are engaged in your own business and, if so, whether the business is a sole proprietorship, partnership or corporation;

2. If you are employed, who is your present employer, how much do you earn and when are your wages paid;
3. Do you receive any interest in your employer's business as part of your compensation;
4. Do you receive any income from a trust fund;
5. Do you receive royalties from any patent, copyright, or invention;
6. Do you receive any support from anyone else, and if so, from whom and how much;
7. Give the names and addresses of all banks in which you have accounts;
8. Identify all certificates of deposit, money market accounts, or other accounts where you have money.
9. Are you holding any real estate mortgages or other notes (does anyone owe *you* money);
10. Do you have an interest in a time-share, condominium or cooperative apartment;
11. List your household furnishings, the present value, and whether money is owed against them;
12. Do you have any valuable collections, i.e. stamp, coin, antiques, or other;
13. Do you own any jewelry and, if so, what is the value;
14. Do you own any automobile(s), boats, airplanes, motor home, etc.;
15. Are you are stockholder in a corporation and, if so, the name of the corporation and the number of shares of stock you own;
16. Do you own any bonds or other securities and, if so, give description;
17. Do you have an IRA, Keogh, pension, or any other retirement funds;
18. Do you have a life insurance policy with a cash surrender value;
19. Are you the beneficiary of a life insurance policy;
20. Are you the beneficiary under a will of someone who has died, or do you otherwise expect to inherit money or property;
21. Is any money held in trust for you;
22. Are you expecting a refund on state or federal income taxes paid.

The creditor may also ask to see your latest tax returns, and any other records regarding your income and expenses. The purpose, of course, is to determine what property you own which the judgment creditor can attach or take to satisfy the judgment. You must respond to the creditor's request or you may be held in contempt of court. Be careful to answer truthfully, as the penalties for perjury may be far greater than the cost of paying your judgment creditor.

When the Creditor Knows What Assets You Have

Once the creditor has obtained information about your assets, he has several options. For example, a judgment creditor may proceed by garnishing your wages, by seizing an asset, such as a car or boat (provided another creditor doesn't have a prior or superior claim to the asset), and selling it, or seizing a bank account.

Some (or all) of your property may be "exempt" from judgment creditors and the creditor may, by law, be prohibited from taking it. These exemptions are explained in greater detail in Chapter 14. You must be given notice when a judgment creditor is attempting to take your property. The notice should explain how you can file a claim for exemption of the property. The judgment creditor will then either withdraw the attachment or ask for a court hearing.

You are entitled to a hearing to explain to the court that the property is exempt or that it is a basic necessity for you. (For example, if you have a vehicle specially equipped for you due to medical reasons, you will want to explain to the court that the vehicle is absolutely necessary for you to carry out your day-to-day activities such as grocery shopping.)

If you lose the first hearing and your situation changes for the worse, you can ask for a second hearing to explain the change in circumstances to the court and the reasons why the attachment should be withdrawn.

Garnishments

Garnishment is a procedure used by judgment creditors which results in loss of control over your disposable earnings. Under the Consumer Credit Protection Act garnishment is defined as any legal or equitable procedure through which the earnings of any individual are required to be withheld for payment of any debt. However, a creditor can also garnish other property such as bank accounts. Wage garnishments are the most common.

Wage garnishments

Congress has enacted laws, contained in the Consumer Credit Protection Act, Sections 1671 through 1677, that restrict the amount of money a creditor can take through garnishment. These laws apply strictly to wages. Congress reasoned that, if garnishment were freely allowed, creditors would unscrupulously encourage the extension of credit, and repayments would take an excessive portion of one's income, thereby creating economic havoc. Garnishments also often result in loss of employment, which has a negative effect on the national economy.

The intent of the law was to grant exemption to wage earners from burdensome garnishments, to protect employment of wage earners, and to prevent bankruptcies. Your state may have its own exemptions. If your state's garnishment laws are even more restrictive, resulting in smaller garnishments, then the state's laws will take priority over the Federal laws; if the state's laws are less restrictive, then the Federal laws will apply.

After a judgment is rendered against you by a court of law, your creditor may attempt to garnish your wages. The method of garnishment varies somewhat from state to state, but it is generally available to most creditors to collect money owed them. (Some states allow garnishments before a judgment is actually entered by the court; however, the procedure must be strictly followed by the creditor as with pre-judgment attachments.)

The Garnishment Procedure — Generally

A notice to withhold a certain amount from your wages is first sent to your employer (see Writ of Garnishment form at the end of this Chapter). In legal terminology the creditor may now be called the "garnishor." The employer may now be referred to as the "garnishee." The garnishee has a certain period of time in which to respond to the notice ordering the garnishee to pay over to the garnishor certain funds which would otherwise belong to you.

The garnishee may, for example, respond by stating that, to the best of his knowledge, you are the head of a household and that therefore your wages are exempt from creditors. Once the response is received by the garnishor, the garnishor will then decide whether the garnishment should be pursued. This may require a court order. If the garnishment remains intact, then the garnishee must turn the property over to the garnishor. This method of collecting on a judgment is often used as a last resort by creditors, as it is time-consuming and can be expensive.

Federal Exemptions From Wage Garnishment

In some states the wages of a head of household cannot be garnished at all; in others only a small percentage of the net pay can be garnished. Under Federal law, which applies if it is more restrictive than your state's garnishment law, the restrictions on garnishment are as follows:

> The aggregate disposable earnings (compensation for services) which are subject to garnishment cannot exceed 25 per cent of the wage earner's disposable

earnings for that week, *or* cannot exceed the amount by
which the wage earner's disposable earnings for that
week exceed thirty times the Federal minimum hourly
wage, whichever is less. If the earnings are paid other
than on a weekly basis, a multiple of the Federal
minimum hourly wage equivalent is prescribed by the
Secretary of Labor.

The restrictions don't apply in the case of a court order for support
order, a filing under Chapter 13 of the Bankruptcy Law (wager-earners
plan), or any debt due for federal or state taxes. If you are supporting
a spouse or dependent children, the maximum amount of disposable
earnings subject to garnishment to enforce a support order (for another
spouse or children) is 50 per cent. If you are not then currently
supporting a spouse or dependent children, then 60 per cent of the
disposable earnings are subject to garnishment to enforce a support
order.

If a support garnishment (garnishment of wages to enforce judgment ordering support) has priority and results in the withholding of
25 per cent or more of your disposable earnings, another creditor
garnishment may not be permitted.

Depending upon your state's laws, filing of a new garnishment
action may be required each time the garnishor wishes to collect money,
and, if so, satisfaction of the creditor's judgment becomes a long and
tedious process.

The restrictions under the Act apply only to wage garnishments,
and not to assignments. If you have assigned a portion of your wages
to a creditor, the assignment is not subject to the percentage limitations.
If you are potentially subject to having your wages or property garnished, you should make it a point to find out exactly how much of your
wages can be garnished and at what time intervals. See Chapter 14 for
state by state wage exemptions.

Restrictions on Discharge From Employment
as a Result of Garnishment

To protect against hardships and disruptions resulting from garnishment of wages, the Federal law has also placed restrictions upon
employers. Under the Federal law, no employer may discharge any
employee for the reason that the employee's earnings have been subject
to garnishment for any one indebtedness. However, this does not
protect you if your wages have been garnished for more than one debt.

If the employer violates the law, he may be subject to a fine of up to
$1,000.00 and imprisonment of up to one year, or both. You may also file
a civil action against the employer.

Wage garnishments under Federal law are regulated by the U.S. Department of Labor.

Non-Wage Garnishments

The judgment creditor may also garnish other money which is due you, such as checking account balances and savings accounts. When a bank is served with a garnishment directed at a depositor's account, the bank isn't required to determine the depositor's right to a wage earner's exemption under the Act, and isn't required to calculate the amount of the exemption before honoring the garnishment. In other words, the entire account, or the amount thereof required to satisfy the judgment, can be garnished.

Writ of Execution and Levy

The judgment against you may have to be recorded in the public records before the creditor can take any further action. For example, it may not be sufficient for a creditor to get a judgment against you in order for that judgment to appear as a lien against your real property. The judgment may also have to be filed in the county recorder's office. (If the creditor obtained his judgment in another state or county, there may be certain procedural requirements the creditor must meet in order for the judgment to be valid where the creditor is attempting to collect it.) If a judgment creditor attempts to attach property, you should determine whether the judgment was properly recorded. If not, you may have a defense to enforcement of the order authorizing the attachment (at least temporarily).

Upon the request of the judgment creditor, the court can enter an order (often included in the final judgment) granting a writ of execution. The writ of execution serves as a lien against your property, and is good through the life of the judgment. (Judgments remain as liens on your property for three to twenty years, depending upon the state in which the judgment was entered. Most are valid between ten and twenty years.) The property subject to the writ of execution may include property acquired *after* the writ of execution has been signed by the court. (In other words, property you get *after* the judgment is entered may also be taken to pay the judgment amount.) The writ of execution may also contain instructions to the sheriff or other law enforcement officials to "levy" or take the property identified in the writ of execution. A "levy" is the absolute legal taking of the property levied on for the payment of a judgment debt. (There are samples of several types of writs at the end of this Chapter. Although the form used in your particular state may vary somewhat, the intent remains the same.)

The sheriff is required to take as much property as is necessary to satisfy the judgment. Except for real estate, the sheriff must take the property into his possession. If the sheriff breaks into your residence to take the property, he should have a court order to do so. Otherwise, he can only enter your residence peacefully (with your consent).

The property is then sold, and the proceeds used to pay the judgment. To avoid the levy, the law may allow you to make payment in full on the writ. As mentioned above, you can also appeal to the court explaining that the property is essential for your livelihood. Once the property is taken, then the sheriff is responsible for its loss or destruction.

Forced sale of certain property will be prohibited by law if the property is exempt (see Chapter 14).

Attachment of Property Not Yet in Your Possession

The judgment creditor can ask the court for an order allowing him to intercept property which would otherwise come to you, such as a tax refund, commissions, or royalties. You must be given notice of the hearing and you have the right to explain to the court why the order should not be entered. If it is ordered in spite of your efforts, then a copy is sent to the person holding the property, such as your real estate broker or publisher, and the payments are then made directly to the judgment creditor.

Attachment of Property Before Judgment

An attachment is a special proceeding authorizing a creditor to take your property *before* he gets a judgment if the creditor believes you will attempt to delay the court proceedings for collection, that you will move the assets out of reach of the creditor, or that you have an intent to defraud the creditor.

Under normal circumstances a creditor may not attach your property without first obtaining a judgment and then a writ of execution as described previously. However, if the creditor has reason to believe that the property will be removed from the court's reach, the court may order the property to be attached.

> **Example:** The sellers of a restaurant sued the buyers for breach of contract, but no final judgment had yet been ordered by the court. The sellers were able to have the buyers' property attached for the reason that the buyers were about to leave the state.

In order to take your property before a judgment is entered, the creditor must post a bond, file an affidavit with the court stating why the property should be attached, and a writ of attachment must be issued by a court of law. To avoid having your property attached, you also have an opportunity to post a bond which will pay the judgment amount if in fact a judgment is entered. After the property is attached, there must be a hearing at which the grounds for the attachment must be proven by the creditor. If you can prove to the court that you are not intending to move the property from the court's reach, that you are not intending to move from the state, and that you have no intention of defrauding your creditor, then the court should release the writ of attachment.

The legal procedure whereby property is taken before a judgment is actually entered must be carefully followed by a creditor. As a debtor, you may have a defense that the constitutional requirements of due process were not met before the property was taken. (The due process requirements include the filing of the creditor's affidavit with the court, the filing of a bond by the creditor, the issuance by the court of a writ of attachment, and the opportunity for the debtor to post a bond.)

For Further Research

Read your state's statutes regarding the legal procedure for collection of a judgment, including garnishment, levy and attachment, noting the maximum time periods allowed for the various steps in the process. When you research your state's statutes, ask the librarian for an "annotated" version. This will include cases which might help clarify certain provisions of the law. The cases will also give you an idea of what kinds of defenses other people in situations similar to yours have presented to the court.

The Federal exemptions from garnishment are found in Title 15, United States Code Annotated, Chapter 41, Subchapter II, Restrictions on Garnishment, Sections 1671 through 1677.

Chapter 13
Bankruptcy as an Option

What is Bankruptcy?

Bankruptcy is a legal and legitimate method of wiping out most, if not all, of your debts. Bankruptcy is usually considered a last resort for credit problems, but if there is no foreseeable change in your income and you are likely to lose everything because of insurmountable debt, then it may be your best alternative. The bankruptcy laws were enacted to give people overwhelmed with debt an opportunity for a fresh start, and if you are at the point of considering bankruptcy as a real possibility, then you should keep this in mind. It is also important to note that only certain debts, commonly referred to a unsecured debts, can be eliminated by a bankruptcy proceeding. The two most common are debts related to medical treatments and credit cards.

Other than the exempt property used to pay current debts, the law assumes you have no resources when you file for bankruptcy. If, for example, you own a vehicle worth $8,000, and the exemption allowed by your state is $1,000, then the bankruptcy court will require that the vehicle be sold and used to pay your unsecured debts. In this case, the loss of your property may not be worth using the bankruptcy process to eliminate your debt.

Congress, in the Bankruptcy Reform Act of 1994, has also made it more difficult for an ex-spouse to use bankruptcy. For example, debts incurred in separation or divorce can no longer be eliminated. These include debts one party owes to another through a property settlement, and debts one party agreed to pay as part of a divorce. Alimony and child support are priority debts which must be paid first.

If a credit card was used to pay income taxes, the credit card debt cannot then be eliminated through bankruptcy.

Types of Bankruptcy

There are several types of bankruptcies for individuals: Chapter 7, Chapter 11 and Chapter 13. Bankruptcy under Chapter 7 discharges your debts, and at the end of the process you are debt-free. Chapter 11 Bankruptcy allows you to act as your own trustee and reorganize your debts. Bankruptcy under Chapter 13, sometimes called a "wage earners bankruptcy," allows you to work out a payment plan whereby you pay back your creditors all or part of the amount you owe them over a period of time.

Bankruptcy, while it won't necessarily terminate foreclosure proceedings, can give you months and sometimes years before you actually lose your property. Even if you file one day before the foreclosure sale, the process is immediately stopped. The lender can ask the Bankruptcy court to allow the foreclosure to proceed—you still have the claims and/or defenses available to you as detailed in Chapter 9.

How Bankruptcy Works

Chapter 7

Under Chapter 7, your assets are generally liquidated to pay the creditors. When the petition in bankruptcy court is filed, all creditors are notified. Once notified, the creditor *cannot* contact you directly about your debt, but must file a claim with the bankruptcy trustee. The creditor *cannot* file a lawsuit against you after receiving notice of your bankruptcy, nor can the creditor continue to pursue any existing lawsuit. The bankruptcy trustee appointed by the court will hold a meeting of your creditors to allow the creditors to ask questions regarding the debt owed to them. The trustee will also take all of your assets over and above those you are allowed by law to keep ("exempt" assets), and sell them. The proceeds of the sale will be used to pay the trustee for his services, any administrative expenses, and ultimately your creditors. (In most cases there is no money left to pay the creditors.) If there are no objections to your bankruptcy filed with the court, an order will then be entered discharging you from all your debts.

If you do not cooperate with the bankruptcy trustee or comply with a court order, or if your debts are consumer debts and you could pay them off with modest effort between three to five years, then your request for a discharge may be denied by the court. However, as a practical matter most people who file under Chapter 7 are granted a discharge in bankruptcy.

Chapter 13

Under this Chapter, creditors are also notified and must stop all action against you to collect their debts. You must work out a payment plan for your creditors, proposing to pay back all or a prorata share of the amount due them. All of your creditors must agree to the repayment plan. Once you have made all of the payments according to your plan, the court will discharge you from those debts.

Chapter 11

Until a 1991 U. S. Supreme Court Ruling, only business entities could file under this Chapter, but now it can be applied to individuals. Unlike Chapters 7 or 13, a trustee isn't automatically appointed, and you can remain in control of your property with the duties and powers exercised by a trustee under Chapters 7 and 13. Filing under Chapter 11 requires a plan to organize your debts, and allows you to continue your business operation.

Bankruptcy Will Not Eliminate All of Your Debts

Bankruptcy will not eliminate all of your debts. Any recent debts owed to the Internal Revenue Service are not dischargeable, nor are most alimony or child support payment orders. Obligations owed as a result of criminal or fraudulent actions, and certain types of student loans are not debts dischargeable in bankruptcy. A debt owed to any creditor you fail to notify of the bankruptcy is not discharged.

The Bankruptcy Court Will Not Take All of Your Property

Under the federal Bankruptcy law and state laws certain property is exempt and cannot be used by the trustee to satisfy your creditors. These exemptions vary from state to state. However, your state exemptions may apply in lieu of the federal bankruptcy exceptions.

The federal Bankruptcy law exemptions can only be used in Connecticut, the District of Columbia, Hawaii, Massachusetts, Michigan, Minnesota, New Jersey, New Mexico, Pennsylvania, Rhode Island, Texas, Vermont, Washington, and Wisconsin. These states also have their own exemptions, but you need to decide whether the federal or state exemptions will allow you to keep more of your property. If you do not live in one of the states listed above, you can only use your state law exemptions. The federal Bankruptcy exemptions are:

- Your right to receive:
    1. A social security benefit, unemployment compensation, or local public assistance benefit;
    2. A veteran's benefit;
    3. A disability, illness or unemployment benefit;
    4. Alimony, support, or separate maintenance payments to the extent reasonably necessary for you and/or your dependents' support;
    5. A payment under a stock bonus, pension, profit-sharing, annuity, or similar plan or contract on account of illness, disability, death, age, or length of service, to the extent reasonably necessary for you and/or your dependents' support, unless
        (i) the plan or contract was established by someone who employed you at the time your rights under the plan accrued;
        (ii) the plan is on account of your age and length of service; *and*
        (iii) the plan doesn't qualify under certain provisions of the Internal Revenue Code.
- Your homestead, including a mobile home or cooperative apartment, to the extent of $7,500.00.
- Any unused portion of the $7,500.00 homestead exemption to the extent of $3,750 may be applied to any other property.
- Personal property including clothing, appliances, furnishings, household goods to $200 each and a total of $4,000.00.
- Tools of trade (for use in your business) to the extent of $750.00.
- A motor vehicle to the extent of $1,200.00.
- Wrongful death recoveries for a person you depended on.
- Personal injury awards to the extent of $7,500.00 (plus damages for pain and suffering and dollar loss).
- Jewelry to $500.00
- Health aids
- Crime victims compensation.
- Life insurance policy with loan value in accrued dividends or interest up to $4,000.00.
- Unmatured life insurance contract, except credit insurance policy.

Only payments reasonably necessary for support are exempt. The bankruptcy law is concerned with your present, not future, security, and thus will generally not exempt savings plans unless you are receiving current income from them.

If you use your state's exemptions, then you may also use these federal non-bankruptcy exemptions:

- Retirement benefits as follows: social security, veteran's benefits, railroad workers benefits, military service employee benefits, military honor roll pensions, foreign service employee pensions, civil service and CIA employee benefits;
- Survivor's benefits of U.S. judges, court directors, judicial center directors, supreme court chief justice administrators;
- Death and disability benefits for military service, war risk hazard injury or death compensation;
- Miscellaneous benefits such as military group life insurance, the greater of 75% of your weekly net income or $114.00 per week, military deposits into a savings account while you are on permanent duty outside the United States, railroad workers unemployment insurance, and seaman's contract wages while at sea.

State homestead and garnishment exemptions are discussed more in the next chapter of this book.

In a Chapter 7 case, you may decide that you need your car or other property on which you owe money. Rather than have the creditor take the property and have the Bankruptcy court discharge your debt to that creditor, you may be able to "reaffirm" that particular debt. By reaffirming the debt, you are making a commitment to that creditor that you will continue the payments. Both the creditor and the Bankruptcy trustee must approve your request to reaffirm any debt.

What Are the Pros and Cons?

Opinions vary as to the effect of a discharge in bankruptcy. Most experts agree that bankruptcy should be used only as a last resort, primarily because of the negative effect it may have on your credit record. The bankruptcy filing will stay in the credit reporting agency's file for a period of ten years. If you are at the point of considering bankruptcy, then your credit report probably isn't very high on your list of priorities.

The primary concern of most people who are considering bankruptcy is the inability to get credit after discharge. However, with the large number of bankruptcy filings, some lenders are changing their attitudes. Once all your debts are discharged, you have that much more disposable income with which to repay a loan. The fact that you have more money available and cannot file Chapter 7 bankruptcy again for another six years may provide the lender a certain level of comfort in giving you a loan.

Finally, many individuals and businesses are now filing for protection from creditors under the Bankruptcy laws. Although feelings of guilt and failure are often associated with Bankruptcy, remember that the primary purpose of the law is to provide a fresh start.

How to File for Bankruptcy

You can file for bankruptcy with the assistance of an attorney. The attorney's fee must be disclosed in the bankruptcy petition. You can also file for bankruptcy on your own. Before attempting to file your own bankruptcy, you should familiarize yourself with the forms and procedures. *How to File Your Own Bankruptcy (or How to Avoid It)* is a self-help guide written by Attorney Edward Haman listing all the exemptions, state by state. It is available from Sphinx Publishing, P.O. Box 25, Clearwater, Florida 34617 for $19.95, plus $2.50 shipping (Florida residents include sales tax). For credit card orders call 1-800-226-5291.

For Further Research

The full text of the Bankruptcy Laws are found at Title 11, United States Code. The exemptions are found at Title 11, United States Code, Section 522.

Chapter 14
Property Exempt from Creditors

As explained in Chapter 13, the Bankruptcy Act prohibits certain property (exempt property) from being taken by the Bankruptcy trustee to satisfy your debts. (In a Bankruptcy either your state or the Bankruptcy Act exemptions will apply.) In other words, you will be able to keep the exempt property even though you have filed for and been discharged by the Bankruptcy Court.

There are also federal and state laws which exempt certain property from judgment creditors. In this case, exempt property is that property which a creditor will not be able to take to satisfy a judgment even if you do not file for bankruptcy. The federal exemptions which you may claim, except for seaman's clothing, involve strictly monetary benefits. The Federal non-bankruptcy exemptions are set forth in the previous Chapter.

The state exemptions may include your homestead (most states allow only a certain portion of the equity to be exempt), a specified portion of your wages, pension and unemployment benefits, public assistance, insurance benefits, tools you must use in your business, and a certain amount of personal property. In some states, if property is owned by you *and* your spouse, and a judgment is entered against only one of you, the jointly-owned property may be unavailable to judgment creditors. (Sixteen states recognize "tenancy by the entirety" property owned by husband and wife, which is exempt from the creditors of only one spouse. See Homestead Exemptions at the end of this Chapter.)

You should be aware of and understand your state's exemptions to determine exactly what property may be taken from you for the payment of debts. (California has two alternative lists of exemptions.) You will need this information in order to complete the personal financial assessment in the next chapter. Also, property given as collateral for a loan is not exempt to the extent of the loan, even though it might be listed as an exemption in your state.

Two of the most important exemptions available—your home and your wages, are listed at the end of this Chapter state by state. Information about additional exemptions available in your state may be obtained at your local library or the state attorney's office. (Most are included in the statutes listed immediately below the name of your state on the attached lists.) They are also listed in *How to File Your Own Bankruptcy (or How to Avoid It)* published by Sphinx Publishing. Remember that the homestead exemption protects your equity in the property to the dollar amount specified by law in your particular state—it does not protect you against foreclosure of a mortgage or loan for which the property was given as collateral.

You should also check with your local court clerk or recorder's office whether or not you must record a statement in the public records listing your exempt property and claiming the exemption, and whether your statement must be published. If at all possible you should be sure that any required filing is done *before* a lawsuit is filed against you or your property is attached. A sample declaration of homestead used in Florida is included at the end of this Chapter.

If you are in doubt as to whether property a creditor is trying to take from you is exempt, go ahead and assert the exemption as a defense. If the creditor contests your claim, the court will decide. It is better to make the attempt and be refused an exemption, than to allow the creditor to take property you should be able to keep.

State by State Homestead Exemptions

Your homestead is your dwelling, with its land and buildings occupied by you as a home, and exempted by law from seizure or sale for a debt. The extent of the homestead varies from state to state. For a more detailed explanation, you should read the statute referenced below your state's name. In addition, your state may be one which recognizes title held by a husband and wife as "tenants by the entireties." If so, it is likely that, as to the property to which title is held in that manner, the property will be exempt from collection for the debts of only one spouse. Among the states which recognize tenants by the entireties are: Florida, Maryland, Indiana, Missouri, North Carolina, Pennsylvania, Ohio, Tennessee, Vermont, Virginia and Wyoming.

Alabama 6-10-2	$5,000 value property, up to 160 acres (separate exemptions for husband and wife).
Alaska 9.38.010	Value to $54,000 based upon percentage ownership in the property; if more than one owner, the aggregate exemptions for one living unit cannot exceed $54,000.
Arizona 33-1101 33-1101(c)	$100,000 in real property, apartment or mobile home plus land; if you sell, proceeds are exempt for up to 18 months.
Arkansas Constitution 9-3, 9-3 & 9-5; 16-66-210	For head of family, unlimited value; 1 acre (not to be reduced to less than 1/4 acre in town), 160 acres (not to be reduced to less than 80 acres) elsewhere, $2,500 value. For others, $800 if single, $1,250 if married. (If in city, 160 acres still applies if property remains rural in nature.)
California 704.720 704.730 703.140(b)(1)	Property to $50,000 if not disabled & single; $75,000 for families if no other member has a homestead; $100,000 if 65 or older, mentally or physically disabled; $100,000 if 55 or older, single & earn under $15,000 or married and earn under $20,000 and creditors force sale of home. Sale proceeds are exempt for six months. (California has two alternative exemption lists—the second list exempts real or personal property to $7,500.)

Colorado 38-41-201 38-41-201.6 13-54-102.5	Real property to $30,000, net of liens, including mobile home or manufactured home; sale proceeds exempt.
Connecticut 52-352(b)	Real property or mobile home up to $75,000.
Delaware 10.4901	None (some personal articles exempt).
District of Columbia	None.
Florida 222.05 Const. 10-4	Unlimited value; up to 1/2 acre in a municipality and 160 acres elsewhere.
Georgia 44-13-100	Interest in property used as residence to $5,000.
Hawaii 36-651-91&92 651-96	Cannot exceed one acre. Head of household or over age 65, value to $30,000; all others, $20,000. Proceeds exempt for six months.
Idaho 55-1003 55-1004	Lesser of $50,000 value, or total net value of all lands, mobile home improvements; sale proceeds exempt for one year.
Illinois 110-12-901 110-12-906	Property occupied as residence value to $7,500; sale proceeds exempt for one year.
Indiana 34-2-28-1 1(a) & 1(b)	Value to $7,500 for each debtor; homestead and personal property exemptions can't exceed $10,000.
Iowa 499A.18 561.2 & 561.16	Within city, 1/2 acre, 40 acres elsewhere, & individual apartment up to $500 value.
Kansas 60-2301 Const. Art.15-9	Unlimited value; 1 acre in town, 160 acres elsewhere.

Kentucky 427-060 427-090	Property value to $5,000; sale proceeds exempt.
Louisiana 20:1	Value to $15,000; maximum 160 acres on one tract, or two or more tracts if home on one and field, garden or pasture on others.
Maine 14-4422	Value to $12,500 (includes burial plot); if you are 60 or over, or mentally or physically disabled (unable to work for at least 12 months) to $60,000.
Maryland	None.
Massachusetts 188-1, 1A	Value to $100,000. If over 62, $200,000, provided an elderly or disabled persons declaration of homestead protection is filed with supporting documentation.
Michigan MCLA 600.1823, 559.214, 700.285	Value to $3,500; 1 lot in town, 40 acres elsewhere.
Minnesota 510.01 & .02 550.37	1/2 acre in town, 160 acres elsewhere (mobile home included), to $200,000, or to $500,000 if for agricultural use; proceeds are exempt.
Mississippi 85-3-21 Miss Const. Sec. 94	Value to $75,000; to 160 acres; sale proceeds exempt.
Missouri 513.430 513.475 513.430(6)	Real property value to $8,000; mobile home used as principal residence, to $1,000.
Montana 70-32-101 & 70-32-104 25-13-614	Value to $40,000; sale proceeds exempt 18 months; 1/4 acre in town, 320 acres outside.
Nebraska 40-101 40-113	Value to $10,000; maximum 2 lots in city, 160 acres elsewhere; sale proceeds exempt 6 months.

Nevada 21.090(M), 21.090(E) 115.010	Value to $95,000, whether or not situated on property owned by debtor; miner's cabin to $4,500.
New Hampshire 480:1	Real property to $30,000 (does not include mobile home).
New Jersey 2A:17-17	None.
New Mexico 42-10-9	Real property to $30,000 if married, widowed or supporting another (if jointly owned, exemption may be doubled).
New York Civil Practice Law & Rules 5206	Real property, co-op, condo or mobile home value to $10,000.
North Carolina 1C-1601 Const. X-2	Value to $10,000 in a residence.
North Dakota 47-18-01 47-18-14	Value to $80,000. Proceeds exempt.
Ohio 2329.66	Residence value to $5,000.
Oklahoma 31-2(1) 31-2(2) 31-2	$5,000 on one acre in city or on 160 acres (one or more parcels) elsewhere (not to be reduced to less than 1/4 acre regardless of value.
Oregon 23.164, 23.164(1) 23.164(5), 23.250 23.240, 23.242	$25,000 ($33,000 if joint ownership); $23,000 ($30,000 if joint ownership) for mobile home & land; if land not owned, mobile home exemption (includes "houseboat") is $20,000 ($27,000 if joint ownership); land limited to 1 block in city, 160 acres elsewhere; sale proceeds exempt 1 year if buying another home.
Pennsylvania	None.
Rhode Island	None.

South Carolina 15-41-30	Residence value to $5,000 (Aggregate of multiple exemptions on same property is $10,000).
South Dakota 43-31-1,2&4	Real property to unlimited value, including mobile home if 240 or more square feet and registered 6 mos. before claim of exemption; 1 acre in town, 160 elsewhere; proceeds to $30,000 (unlimited if over age 70) exempt for 1 year.
Tennessee 26-2-301	Value to $5,000; $7,500 if joint ownership (to be equally divided if there are simultaneous claims).
Texas 41.001 & .002	Unlimited value; 1 acre in town, 100 acres (200 if family) elsewhere; sale proceeds exempt for 6 months.
Utah 78-23-3	Property to value of $8,000 for head of household; add $2,000 for spouse and $500 per dependent.
Vermont T.27-101	Residence and land value to $30,000.
Virginia 34-4	Property value to $5,000, plus $500 for each dependent; additional exemption for certain veterans.
Washington 6.13.010 & .180	Property value to $30,000; proceeds exempt.
West Virginia 38-10-4, 38-9-3	Residence value to $7,500, ($7500 in bankruptcy).
Wisconsin 815.20	Residence value to $40,000; sale proceeds exempt for 2 years if you're buying another home.
Wyoming 1-20-101 & 104	Residence value to $10,000; house trailer to $6,000.

State by State Garnishment Exemptions

Wages are payments for services rendered by an individual. For the purposes of determining the amount of your wage exemption, generally only the amount of your disposable (after tax and withholding) earnings are considered wages. The information provided below is merely a brief outline. The amount or percentage shown is that amount which is exempt from garnishment, i.e. not available to creditors to satisfy a debt.

Where the exempt amount is based upon a multiple of the Federal minimum hourly wage (Title 29 USC 106 (a)(1)), and you are paid on other than a weekly basis, the multiples must be adjusted based upon your pay period. Please note that in cases where wages are being garnished for money due under a support order, the exempt amount may be substantially reduced (a larger amount will be available to the creditor).

You should read your state statute shown below the state name to help you in calculating the exact amount of your wage exemption, and for a listing of other income and property which may be beyond the reach of your creditors.

Alabama 6-10-7	75% of your weekly wage, salary or compensation is exempt.
Alaska 9.38.030 9.38.050 938.015 938.025	Weekly net earnings to $350; for sole household wage earner, $550. If you don't get paid monthly, semi-monthly or weekly, then you can claim $1,400 in cash or liquid assets paid in any month; the sole wage earner can claim $2,200; including disability benefits.
Arizona 33-1131(B)	Either 75% of your weekly net earnings or 30 times the Federal minimum hourly wage, whichever is greater, is exempt (only half are exempt if the garnishment is for support).
Arkansas 16-66-208	Any earned but unpaid wages due for 60 days, but $25 per week is absolutely exempt.
California 704.113 704.070	75% of your wages paid within 30 days before a writ is issued are exempt, (all wages are exempt if before payment they were subject to a withholding order or wage assignment for support).

Colorado 13-54-104	Either 75% of your weekly net earnings or 30 times the Federal minimum hourly wage, whichever is greater, is exempt.
Connecticut 52-361(a)	Either 75% of your weekly net earnings or 40 times the Federal minimum hourly wage, whichever is greater, is exempt.
Delaware 10-4913	85% of your unpaid wages or other remuneration.
District of Columbia 16-572	Either 75% of your weekly net earnings or 30 times the Federal minimum hourly wage, whichever is greater, is exempt.
Florida 222.11	Wages are exempt if head of household.
Georgia 18-4-20 18-4-21	Either 75% of your weekly net earnings or 30 times the Federal minimum hourly wage, whichever is greater, is exempt.
Hawaii 36-651-121	Unpaid wages due for services of past 31 days immediately before writ of garnishment are exempt.
Idaho 11-207	Either 75% of your weekly net earnings or 30 times the Federal minimum hourly wage, whichever is greater, is exempt.
Illinois 110-12-803	Either 85% of your weekly net earnings or 45 times the Federal minimum hourly wage, whichever is greater, is exempt.
Indiana 24-4.5-5-105 2(a) & (b)	Either 75% of your weekly net earnings or 30 times the Federal minimum hourly wage, whichever is greater, is exempt.
Iowa 642.21	If earnings less than $12,000 per year, maximum subject to garnishment is $250 per year per judgment creditor (increase graduated with increase in wages). Exemptions as under Federal Consumer Credit Protection Act, Title III, 15 USC 1671-1677.

Kansas 60-2310	Either 75% of your weekly net earnings or 30 times the Federal minimum hourly wage, whichever is greater, is exempt.
Kentucky 427.010	Either 75% of your weekly net earnings or 30 times the Federal minimum hourly wage, whichever is greater, is exempt.
Louisiana 13.3881	Either 75% of your weekly net earnings or 30 times the Federal minimum hourly wage, whichever is greater, is exempt.
Maine 14-3127(1)	Either 75% of your weekly net earnings or 40 times the Federal minimum hourly wage, whichever is greater, is exempt.
Maryland 15-601.1	Either 75% of your weekly net earnings or 30 times the Federal minimum hourly wage, whichever is greater, is exempt in Caroline, Kent, Queen Anne and Worcester Counties; in other counties, greater of 75% of actual wages or $145 per week.
Massachusetts c.246-28	Pension payments being received by Trustee. Unpaid but earned wages up to $125 per week (held by Trustee) are exempt.
Michigan 600-5311	40% of earned but unpaid wages; if head of household, 60%. Head of household may keep at least $15 per week plus $2 for every dependent except spouse; others may keep at least $10 per week.
Minnesota 571.55(2)	Either 75% of your weekly net earnings or 40 times the Federal minimum hourly wage, whichever is greater, is exempt .
Mississippi 85 3-4(2)	100% of wages received for first 30 days after service of writ of garnishment; after 30 days, either 75% of your weekly net earnings or 30 times the Federal minimum hourly wage, whichever is greater, is exempt.
Missouri 525.030	Either 75% of your weekly net earnings or 30 times the Federal minimum hourly wage, whichever is greater, is exempt.

Montana 25-13-614	Either 75% of your weekly net earnings or 30 times the Federal minimum hourly wage, whichever is greater, is exempt.
Nebraska 25-1558	Either 75% (85% for head of household) of your weekly net earnings or 30 times the Federal minimum hourly wage, whichever is greater, is exempt.
Nevada 21-090	Either 75% of your weekly net earnings or 30 times the Federal minimum hourly wage, whichever is greater, is exempt.
New Hampshire 512:21	Fifty times Federal minimum hourly wage on wages earned before the writ of garnishment is served; all wages earned after service of the writ.
New Jersey 2A 17-56	If income is $7,500 or under, 90% of earned but unpaid wages; judge decides exemption if income is over $7,500 (larger percentage may then be garnished).
New Mexico 35-12-7	Either 75% of your weekly net earnings or 40 times the Federal minimum hourly wage, whichever is greater, is exempt.
New York CPLR 5205:2	90% of debtor's income earned within 60 days of attempted garnishment is exempt.
North Carolina 1-362	Earned but unpaid wages received 60 days before writ is issued which are needed for support (as evidenced by affidavit or otherwise) are exempt.
North Dakota 32.09.1-03	Either 75% of your weekly net earnings or 40 times the Federal minimum hourly wage, whichever is greater, is exempt.
Ohio 2329.66(13)(a)	Either 75% of your weekly net earnings or 30 times the Federal minimum hourly wage, whichever is greater, is exempt.
Oklahoma 12-1171.1 31-1	75% of wages earned within 90 days before writ is issued are exempt.

Oregon 23.185	Up to $160 of net weekly earnings is exempt.
Pennsylvania 42-8127	Earned but unpaid wages (wages still in hands of employer) are exempt.
Rhode Island 9-26-4(6) 9-26-4(8)(A) 30-7-9	Wages due or accruing to any seaman are exempt wages, or salary paid from money appropriated for relief of poor or in aid of unemployment are exempt. Salary or wages due debtor, where debtor received relief from governmental agency within one year prior, are exempt. Wages or salary up to $50 are exempt. Salary of wife & minor children are exempt. Pay due or to become due to any member of the militia for active service are is exempt.
South Carolina	None.
South Dakota 15-20-12	Earned wages owed within 60 days before writ of garnishment is served which is needed for family support (as evidenced by affidavit or otherwise) are exempt.
Tennessee 26-2-106 26-2-107	Either 75% of your weekly net earnings or 30 times the Federal minimum hourly wage, whichever is greater, plus $2.50 per week per dependent child under 16, is exempt.
Texas Property 42.002(b)(1)	All earned but unpaid wages are exempt.
Utah 70C-7-103(a)	Either 75% of your weekly net earnings or 30 times the Federal minimum hourly wage, whichever is greater, is exempt.
Vermont 3170, (b)(1), (b)(2)	Either 75% of your weekly net earnings or 30 times the Federal minimum hourly wage, whichever is greater, is exempt. All wages are exempt if you received welfare during 2 months before writ is issued.
Virginia 34-19	Either 75% of your weekly net earnings or 30 times the Federal minimum hourly wage, whichever is greater, is exempt.

Washington 6.27.150	Either 75% of your weekly net earnings or 30 times the Federal minimum hourly wage, whichever is greater, is exempt.
West Virginia 38-5A-3	Either 75% of your weekly net earnings or 30 times the Federal minimum hourly wage, whichever is greater, is exempt.
Wisconsin 815.18	75% of income for each one-week pay period, but not less than 30 times the Federal minimum hourly wage per week, is exempt.
Wyoming 1-15-511(a)	75% of your weekly net earnings or 30 times the Federal minimum hourly wage, whichever is greater, is exempt.

Chapter 15
Personal Assessment and Planning for the Future

Debt and Asset Evaluation

While taking care of your current financial problems you should also be thinking about the future. A job loss or long-term illness is rarely anticipated, but should be considered when making your decisions about how to handle your income and assets. Tough economic times catch most people by surprise—they find they have to do whatever is necessary to get by, including getting family members to pitch in with income from part-time jobs. Saving for a rainy day is always recommended by financial planners—some are now even urging people to have a full year's living expenses available in the event of a major setback.

Saving a full year's living expenses isn't easy when you're just trying to meet your monthly obligations. Making sure your property is safe or exempt from creditors is a step you can begin taking now. Before doing anything, however, make an honest assessment of where you are financially.

To help you better assess your financial situation, you should complete the chart at the end of this chapter. (If you decide to use consumer credit counseling services as mentioned in Chapter 2, you may be required to complete a similar personal financial assessment.) First, you should determine exactly what your income and assets are, versus your liabilities. You may find that you have sufficient income and assets to satisfy your creditors, albeit at a reduced amount, for a period of time until you are again able to fully meet your obligations.

Second, you should determine which of your assets have been given as security for a debt, such as your car, furniture, appliances and, of course, your home. These will be the assets subject to foreclosure or repossession by the creditor.

Third, you should determine which of your assets are currently subject to attachment or levy by a creditor. Perhaps you might consider selling some of these assets to pay down your debt, rather than having a creditor take them to satisfy a judgment.

Making Yourself "Judgment Proof"

Finally, you should consider methods by which you can make yourself "judgment proof." Being "judgment proof" does not mean that a judgment cannot be entered against you—it simply means that anyone who has a judgment against you will be unable to collect it because any property you do own is exempt. As explained in previous chapters, certain property will be exempt from creditors, including judgment creditors and, in some cases, even the IRS.

If you do have assets which you want to keep from potential creditors' hands, you may want to take more drastic measures. For instance, consider moving to a state with exemptions which would allow you to keep those assets. For example, if you have a large amount of cash, you may want to move to a state with an unlimited homestead exemption and put your cash into your homestead.

A FINAL NOTE OF CAUTION: If you are expecting a judgment to be entered against you in the near or immediate future, before transferring property in order to avoid the judgment creditor, contact an attorney. The transfer may be attacked by the creditor as a "fraudulent conveyance." The same holds true if you are thinking about filing bankruptcy. A transfer can be set aside by the bankruptcy court as a preference. **Proper planning in these instances should include sound legal advice.**

Personal Financial Assessment

Net Income (After Taxes):

Source	Monthly Amt.	Non-IRS Exempt? (Y or N)	IRS Exempt? (Y or N)	If Exempt How Much?
Wages				
Social Security				
Pension Fund				
Alimony/Support				
Public Assistance				
Disability				
Other (type)				
TOTALS				*

*The total of the exempt amounts is the amount of income you will be able to keep every month regardless of any judgment collection efforts or garnishments by creditors. If the IRS is among your creditors, make sure you use the third column to determine your exemptions.

Monthly Expenses:

<u>Amount</u>

	Amount
Mortgage/Rent	
Home maintenance	
Homeowners insurance	
Food	
Food away from home	
Gas/Electric	
Water	
Trash Collection	
Phone	
Car payment(s)	
Gas/oil/maintenance	
Car insurance	
Other transportation	
Life insurance	
Health insurance	
School/Books/Tuition	
Child care	
Child Support/Alimony	
Medical expenses	
Clothing	
Subscriptions	
Cable TV	
Dues/Church tithes	
Other	
TOTAL:	$

Your total monthly expenses, deducted from your total net monthly income listed on page 139, should give you an indication of your financial situation. You may be able to reduce or eliminate some of these expenses in order to pay other debts.

Your Assets:

	Value	Equity	$ Amt. of Liens on Property	Non-IRS Exempt? (Y or N)	IRS Exempt? (Y or N)
Homestead					
Other Real Estate					
Automobiles					
Household Goods (Furniture, Appliances)					
Trade Tools					
Other (examples: stocks, bonds, CD's, savings)					
TOTALS					

In calculating the extent to which your property is exempt from creditors, be sure to determine whether the property is owned by you *and* your spouse jointly, and whether you live in a state where the joint property cannot be taken for the debt of only one spouse.

The liens on your property include any loan made to you for which the property was taken as collateral (i.e. a mortgage or car loan), liens which attach to your property by law (such as contractor's liens), or liens which have resulted from judgments entered against you by a court.

The equity is the amount of money that would be left over when the property is sold and the loans against it (secured creditor) is paid. The equity, if not exempt from creditors, is the amount that would then be available to pay your other creditors.

Your financial health will be determined by comparing your monthly income with your monthly expenses, and by evaluating the amount of equity you have (if any) in your property. The "exempt" amounts are what would be left to you if your creditors obtained judgments and took your property as payment, or if you file for bankruptcy.

Below is an additional worksheet to help you in determining your equity in your property. Be honest with yourself when completing the form. Often, owners inflate the value of their property. Remember, what you paid for the property is not necessarily what it is worth, nor will you necessarily be able to sell it for as much as you paid.

Assets Given as Collateral:

Name of Asset	Value	Creditor	Balance of Secured Debt	Equity
House/Real Estate	$		$	$
Other Real Estate	$		$	$
Automobile	$		$	$
Automobile	$		$	$
Furniture	$		$	$
Stereo/Television	$		$	$
Jewelry	$		$	$
Other	$		$	$
Other	$		$	$

If you have assets which are secured, i.e. a mortgage against your house, or a loan against your car, you must remember that the creditor can take the property for payment of the debt. If the property is valuable, and little is owed on your loan, you should consider selling it yourself, paying the creditor, and using the balance left to pay off other debts. If you have little or no equity in the property (the balance due on the loan equals or exceeds the value), consider selling it and asking the creditor to accept the buyer as the new borrower and releasing you from your obligations (unless the buyer can pay cash). Remember, if the creditor takes steps to repossess the property, any costs, including attorneys fees, will be added on the amount you already owe.

Glossary

The following words and phrases are used throughout this book.

Adjudication - The act of a court of law making an order or judgment.

Affidavit - A sworn, written declaration, usually signed before a notary public.

Assignment (of wages or other property) - to transfer an interest in certain property to another.

Bond - a written promise of another (surety) to pay a debt in the event the debtor fails to pay.

Civil Remedies - the legal means of enforcing a civil (as opposed to criminal) right.

Collateral - security (usually property) pledged for the payment of a loan.

Complaint - also called a "Petition," the first document filed in a civil lawsuit.

Compliance - acting in accordance with certain legal requirements.

Damages - the estimate money equivalent of an injury or wrong.

Default - failure to meet an obligation, such as a loan payment or court appearance.

Deficiency/Notice of Deficiency - the amount by which a creditor's claim is not satisfied, and the notice thereof to the debtor.

Disclosure/disclose - the act of revealing certain information, particularly to a debtor regarding his loan.

Equitable Title - the right of ownership, although legal title is held by another.

Equity - the amount of value of property remaining after deducting the mortgage and other pledges or liens rightfully against the property.

Equity Line - a line of credit, or loan, given by a lender with the equity in real estate given as collateral.

Execute/Execution - to carry out the terms of a legal document, esp. a judgment.

Fair Market Value - price at which a willing buyer and willing seller will trade.

Financial Statement - a statement, usually requested by a lender, which describes your property, its value, your income and liabilities (debt), indicating your actual financial condition.

Foreclose/Foreclosure - the termination of all of the rights of the borrower in property given as collateral to the mortgagee or lender.

Governmental Instrumentality - an agency of the government.

Indemnification - act of agreeing to compensate someone for any loss or damage.

Lien - a claim against property for the payment of a debt or obligation.

Mortgage - the pledge of property as security for a loan, usually real property.

Negligence/Negligent - to omit doing something through indifference or carelessness.

Periodic Rates - interest rates which change from time to time as specified in the loan documents.

Personal Property - also referred to a "chattel," any property which is moveable as opposed to real estate or fixed to real estate.

Petition - See "Complaint" above.

Pro Rata - in proportion to something; according to a certain rate.

Public Record - records which are kept by a governmental body and available to the public for review.

Punitive Damages - compensation awarded for an injury or wrong which are intended to punish the one who committed such injury or wrong.

Purchase Money Mortgage - mortgage given by the buyer back to the seller of property.

Quit Claim Deed - transfer of title to real estate which does not contain any guaranties or warranties.

Real Property - real estate, land.

Remedies - the means of enforcing a right.

Repossess - to regain possession of something; also used when the creditor is taking possession of collateral after default in the payments by the debtor.

Residential Mortgage Transaction - transaction with the lender whereby real property is given as collateral in exchange for funds.

Residual Value - the value of property at the end of a specific time period, esp. at the end of a lease term.

Security Interest - an interest in property given as collateral for a debt.

Statutes - a written law which is passed by a governing authority, usually a state legislature or Congress.

Statute of Limitations - a statute stating the period of time in which a claim can be brought before a court.

Superior Claim - a claim against property, usually by a lender, which takes priority over another claim, i.e. which must be paid before another claim against the same property can be paid.

Tenants by the Entireties - a manner of holding title to property by husband and wife, recognized in nearly one-third of all states, whereby each party holds title to the entire property, and it cannot be divided without the consent of both husband and wife.

Underwriting - to assume liability for something to the extent of a certain dollar amount.

Void/voidable - without legal force or effect/to cause to be without legal force or effect.

Writ - a legal document, ordering an authorized person to do a certain act (or to refrain from doing something).

Appendix A
U.S. Government Printing Offices

Information about your rights under the Consumer Credit Protection Act, including Truth-in-Lending and Regulation Z, should be available at the following U.S. Government Bookstores:

Alabama
Birmingham Bookstore,
Roebuck Shopping City,
9220-B Parkway East,
Birmingham, AL
35206,
FTS-229-1056,
Commercial (205) 254-1056

California
Los Angeles Bookstore
ARCO Plaza, C-Level
505 S. Flower St., Los Angeles, CA 90071
FTS-798-5841
Commercial (213) 894-5841

San Francisco Bookstore
Rm. 1023, Federal Bldg.
450 Golden Gate Ave.
San Francisco, CA 94102,
FTS-556-6657
Commercial (415)-556-0643

Colorado
Denver Bookstore
Rm 117, Federal Bldg.
1961 Stout St.,
Denver, CO 80294
FTS-564-3964
Commercial (303) 844-3964

Pueblo Bookstore
World Savings Bldg.
720 N. Main St.
Pueblo, CO 81003
FTS-323-9371
Commercial (303) 544-3142

Pueblo Distribution Center
Pub. Docs. Distribution Center
PO Box 4007
Pueblo, CO 81003
FTS-323-9301
Commercial (303) 948-2240

District of Columbia
Commerce Bookstore
14th & Pennsylvania Ave, NW
Rm. 1604, 1st Fl.
Washington, DC 20230
FTS-377-3527
Commercial (202) 377-3527

Farragut Bookstore
Matomic Bldg.
1717 H. St., NW
Washington, DC 20006,
FTS-653-5075
Commercial (202) 653-5075

Main Bookstore
710 North Capitol St NW
Washington, DC 20401,
FTS-275-2091
Commercial (202)275-2091

Florida
Jacksonville Bookstore
Rm. 158, Federal Bldg.
400 W. Bay St
Jacksonville, FL 32202
FTS-946-3801
Commercial (904) 791-3801

Georgia
Atlanta Bookstore
Rm. 100, Federal Bldg.
275 Peachtree St, NE
Atlanta, GA 30303
FTS-242-6946
Commercial (404)-221-694

Illinois
Chicago Bookstore
Rm 1365, Federal Bldg.
219 S. Dearborn St
Chicago, IL 60604
FTS-353-5133
Commercial (312) 353-5133

Maryland
Laurel Bookstore
8660 Cherry Lane
Laurel, MD 20707
Commercial (301) 953-7974

Massachusetts
Boston Bookstore
Rm G-25, Federal Bldg.
Sudbury St
Boston, MA 02203
FTS- 223-6071
Commercial (617) 223-6071

Michigan
Detroit Bookstore
Suite 160, Federal Bldg.
477 Michigan Ave
Detroit, MI 48226
FTS-226-7816
Commercial (313) 226-7816

Missouri
Kansas City Bookstore
#120 Bannister Mall
5600 East Bannister Rd
Kansas City, MO 64137
FTS-926-7261
Commercial (816) 765-2256

New York
New York Bookstore
Rm. 110, Federal Bldg.
26 Federal Plaza
New York, NY 10278
FTS-264-3825
Commercial (212) 264-3825

Ohio
Cleveland Bookstore
1st Fl., Federal Bldg,
1240 E. 9th St,
Cleveland, OH 44199
FTS-942-4922
Commercial (216) 522-4922

Columbus Bookstore
Rm 207, Federal Bldg.
200 N. High St
Columbus, OH 43215
FTS -943-6956
Commercial (612) 469-6956

Pennsylvania
Philadelphia Bookstore
Robert Morris Bldg.
100 N 17th St
Philadelphia, PA 19102
FTS-597-0677
Commercial (215) 597-0677

Pittsburgh Bookstore
Rm 118, Federal Bldg.
1000 Liberty Ave
Pittsburgh, PA 15222
FTS-722-2721
Commercial (412) 644-2721

Texas
Dallas Bookstore
Rm 1C50, Federal Bldg
1100 Commerce St
Dallas, TX 75242
FTS-729-0076
Commercial (214) 767-0076

Houston Bookstore
45 College Center,
9319 Gulf Freeway
Houston, TX 77017
FTS-526-7515
Commercial (713) 229-3515

Washington
Seattle Bookstore
Rm 194, Federal Bldg.
915 Second Ave
Seattle, WA 98174
FTS -399-4290
Commercial (206) 442-4270

Wisconsin
Milwaukee Bookstore
Rm. 190, Federal Bldg.
517 E. Wisconsin Ave
Milwaukee, WI 53202
FTS-362-1300
Commercial (414) 291-1304

Note. Mail orders can also be sent to:
Superintendent of Documents
Washington, DC 20402

Appendix B
State by State Consumer Affairs Offices

Alabama:
Consumer Protection Division
Office of Attorney General
11 South Union Street
Montgomery, AL 36130
(800) 392-5658; (334) 242-7334

Alaska:
Office of the Attorney General
P.O. Box K
State Capitol
Juneau, AK 99811-0300
(907) 465-3600

Arizona:
Consumer Complaints
Office of the Attorney General
1275 W. Washington St.
Phoenix, AZ 85007
(800) 352-8431; (602)542-5763

Arkansas:
Attorney General's Office
Consumer Protection
200 Tower Building
323 Center Street
Little Rock, AR 72201
(800) 482-8982; (501) 682-2341

California:
Consumer Affairs Office
400 "R" Street, Suite 1040
Sacramento, CA 95814-6200
(800) 952-5210; (916) 445-1254

Colorado:
Consumer Protection Unit
Office of Attorney General
1525 Sherman St., 5th Floor
Denver, CO 80203
(800) 332-2071; (303) 866-5189

Connecticut:
Department of Consumer Protection
165 Capitol Avenue
Hartford, CT 06106
(203) 566-1170

Delaware:
Division of Consumer Affairs
820 North French Street, 4th Fl.
Wilmington, DE 19801
(302) 577-3250

District of Columbia:
Dept. of Consumer
& Regulatory Affairs
614 H Street, N.W., Room 106
Washington, DC 20001
(202) 727-7076

Florida:
Division of Consumer Services
Dept. of Agriculture &
Consumer Services
218 Mayo Building
Tallahassee, FL 32399
(800) 435-7352; (904) 488-2226

Georgia:
Office of Consumer Affairs
2 Martin Luther King Jr. Drive
Plaza Level East
Atlanta, GA 30334
(404) 651-8600

Hawaii:
Office of Consumer Protection
Department of Commerce &
Consumer Affairs
P.O. Box 3767
Honolulu, HI 96812
(808) 586-2630

Idaho:
Consumer Protection Division
Office of Attorney General
Statehouse Room 113A
Boise, ID 83720-1000
(800) 432-3545; (208) 334-2424

Illinois:
Office of Attorney General
Consumer Protection Division
500 South 2nd Street
Springfield, IL 62706
(800) 252-8666; (217) 782-9011

Indiana:
Consumer Protection Division
Office of Attorney General
219 State House
Indianapolis, IN 46204
(800) 382-5516; (317) 232-6330

Iowa:
Consumer Protection Division
Office of Attorney General
1300 East Walnut
Des Moines, A 50319
(515) 281-5926

Kansas:
Office of Attorney General
Consumer Protection Division
301 W. 10th Street
Topeka, KS 66612-1597
(800) 432-2310; (913) 296-3751

Kentucky:
Consumer Protection Division
Office of Attorney General
209 St. Clair Street
Frankfort, KY 40601
(800) 432-9257; (502) 573-2200

Louisiana:
Attn: Consumer Protection Division
Department of Justice
P.O. Box 94095
Baton Rouge, LA 70804
(504) 342-9638

Maine:
Attorney General Consumer
        Mediation Service
State House Station No. 6
Augusta, ME 04333-0035
(800) 332-8529; (207) 582-8718

Maryland:
Consumer Protection Division
200 St. Paul Place
Baltimore, Maryland 21202
(410) 528-8662

Massachusetts:
Exec. Office of Consumer Affairs
One Ashburton Place
Boston, MA 02108

Michigan:
Consumers Protection Division
Office of Attorney General
P.O. Box 30213
Lansing, MI 48909
(517) 373-1140

Minnesota:
Consumer Affairs Division
Office of Attorney General
1400 NCL Tower
445 Minnesota Street
St. Paul, MN 55101
(800) 657-3787; (612) 296-3353

Mississippi:
Consumer Protection Division
Office of Attorney General
P.O. Box 22947
Jackson, MS 39225
(601) 359-4230

Missouri:
Public Protection
Office of Attorney General
P.O. Box 899
Jefferson City, MO 65102
(800) 392-8222; (314) 751-3321

Montana:
Office of Consumer Affairs
Department of Commerce
1424 9th Avenue
Helena, MT 59620
(406) 444-4312

Nebraska:
Office of Attorney General
Consumer Protection Division
2115 State Capitol
Lincoln, NE 68509
(402) 471-2682

Nevada:
Consumer Affairs Division
Department of Consumer Affairs
State Mail Room Complex
Las Vegas, NV 89158
(702) 486-7355

New Hampshire:
Consumer Protection and
    Antitrust Division
Office of Attorney General
State House Annex
Concord, NH 03301
(603) 271-3641

New Jersey:
Office of Consumer Protection
P.O. Box 45027
Newark, NJ 07101
(201) 504-6200

New Mexico:
Consumer Protection Division
Office of the Attorney General
P.O. Drawer 1508
Santa Fe, NM 87504
(800) 678-1508; (505) 827-6910

New York:
State Consumer Protection Board
99 Washington Avenue
Albany, NY 12210
(518) 474-8583

North Carolina:
Consumer Protection Section
Office of Attorney General
P.O. Box 629
Raleigh, NC 27602
(919) 733-7741

North Dakota:
Consumer Fraud Section
Office of Attorney General
600 East Boulevard
Bismarck, ND 58505
(800) 472-2600; (701) 224-3404

Ohio:
Consumer Protection Division
Office of Attorney General
30 East Broad Street, 25th Floor
Columbus, OH 43266-0410
(800) 282-0515; (614) 466-4986

Oklahoma:
Consumer Protection Division
Office of Attorney General
4545 N. Lincoln, Suite 1260
Oklahoma City, OK 73105
(405) 521-4274

Oregon:
Financial Fraud Section
Department of Justice
Justice Building
Salem, OR 97310
(503) 378-4320

Pennsylvania:
Bureau of Consumer Protection
Office of Attorney General
132 Kline Village
Harrisburg, PA 17104
(800) 441-2555; (717) 787-9707

Rhode Island:
Consumer Protection Division
Office of Attorney General
72 Pine Street
Providence, RI 02903
(401) 277-2104

South Carolina:
Department of Consumer Affairs
P.O. Box 5757
Columbia, SC 29250
(800) 922-1594; (803) 734-9452

South Dakota:
Division of Consumer Affairs
Office of Attorney General
State Capitol Building
500 E. Capitol
Pierre, SD 57501
(605) 773-4400

Tennessee:
State of Tennessee
Dept. of Commerce and Insurance
Division of Consumer Affairs
500 James Robertson Pkwy, 5th Floor
Nashville, TN 37243-0600
(800) 342-8385; (615) 741-4737

Texas:
Consumer Protection Division
Office of Attorney General
P.O. Box 12548
Austin, TX 78711
(512)463-2070

Utah:
Division of Consumer Protection
Department of Business Regulation
160 East 300 South
P.O. Box 45804
Salt Lake City, UT 84145-0804
(801) 530-6601

Vermont:
Consumer Assistance Program
Office of Attorney General
104 Morrill Hall
Burlington, VT 05405
(800) 649-2424; (802) 656-3183

Virginia:
Division of Consumer Affairs
Box 1163
Richmond, VA 23209
(800) 552-9963; (804) 786-2042

Washington:
Consumer Protection Division
Office of Attorney General
900 4th Avenue, Room 2000
Seattle, WA 98164
(800) 551-4636; (206) 464-6684

West Virginia:
Consumer Protection Division
Office of Attorney General
812 Quarrier Street, 6th Floor
Charleston, WV 25301
(800) 368-8808; (304) 558-8986

Wisconsin:
Division of Trade and Consumer
   Protection
Department of Agriculture, Trade
   and Consumer Protection
P.O. Box 8911
Madison, WI 53708-8911

Wyoming:
Consumer Affairs Division
Office of Attorney General
123 State Capitol Building
Cheyenne, WY 82002
(307) 777-7841

Appendix C
Federal Trade Commission
Regional Offices

States in Region	Office and Address
Alabama, Florida, Georgia, Mississippi, North Carolina, South Carolina, Tennessee, Virginia	Rm. 1000, 1718 Peachtree St., N.W. Atlanta, Georgia 30367
Connecticut, Maine, Massachusetts, New Hampshire, Rhode Island, Vermont	Rm. 1184, 10 Causeway Street Boston, Massachusetts 02222-1073
Illinois, Indiana, Iowa, Kentucky, Minnesota, Missouri, Wisconsin	Ste. 1437, 55 E. Monroe Street Chicago, Illinois 60603
Michigan, Ohio, Pennsylvania, West Virginia, Delaware, Maryland	Ste. 520-A, 668 Euclid Avenue Cleveland, Ohio 44114
Arkansas, Louisiana, New Mexico, Oklahoma, Texas	Ste. 500, 100 N. Central Expressway Dallas, Texas 75201
Colorado, Kansas, Montana, Nebraska, North Dakota, South Dakota, Utah, Wyoming	Ste. 2900, 1405 Curtis Street Denver, Colorado 80202-2393
Arizona, Southern California	Ste. 13209, 11000 Wilshire Blvd. Los Angeles, California 90024
Northern California, Hawaii, Nevada	Ste. 570, 901 Market Street San Francisco, California 94103
Alaska, Idaho, Oregon, Washington	Room 2806, 915 2nd Avenue Seattle, Washington 98174
New York, New Jersey	13th Floor, 150 William Street New York, New York 10038

Appendix D
Statutes of Limitations

The "Statute of Limitations" is the law which sets the time period in which a lawsuit can be filed after a specified event. The time periods below are all in years. More detailed information follows the listing.

A written contract is one which has been signed by the parties. A promissory note is document which has been signed stating the amount to be paid and the manner in which it is to be paid. The promissory note usually includes a provision for default—i.e. what the creditor or lender can do in the event payment is not made as required in the note. As you will see below, the time period in which a creditor can file a lawsuit to collect on a promissory note is generally the same as the time limitation for suing on a written contract. Only two states, Delaware and Louisiana, set a different time limitation for suing on a promissory note. An oral contract is just that—a verbal agreement to do something which has not been reduced to writing and signed by the parties.

The list is by no means exhaustive. You should consult your state laws for more specific information. Typically, the reference to the Statute of Limitations can be found in the index to your state statutes, under the heading "Limitation of Actions." To get you started, below is a list of some of the statutory references, state by state. However, these include only the limitations listed above. There may be additional and different time limitations for lawsuits on sales contracts, open-end revolving accounts, lawsuits for damages, etc. Also, you will be able to find your state's time limitation for filing a lawsuit to collect a judgment.

State	Written Contracts	Promissory Notes	Oral Contracts	Statutory Reference
Alabama	6	6	6	6-2-33, 6-2-34
Alaska	6	6	6	09.10.050, 45-02-725
Arizona	6	6	3	12-548, 12-543
Arkansas	5	5	3	16-56-115, 16-56-105
California	4	4	2	CCP 337
Colorado	6	6	6	13-80-103.5
Connecticut	6	6	3	52-576, 52-581
Delaware	3	6	3	10-8106, 10-8109
Florida	5	5	4	95.11
				9-3-24, 9-3-25

State	Written Contracts	Promissory Notes	Oral Contracts	Statutory Reference
Georgia	6	6	4	657-1
Hawaii	6	6	6	5-216, 5-217
Idaho	5	5	4	13-206, 13-205
Illinois	10	10	5	34-1-2-1
Indiana	6	6	6	614.1
Iowa	10	10	5	60.511, 60.512
Kansas	5	5	3	413.090, 413.120
Kentucky	15	15	5	CC 3509, 3478
Louisiana	10	5	10	14-751
Maine	6	6	6	CJ 5-101
Maryland	3	3	3	260.2
Massachusetts	6	6	6	600.5813, 451.435
Michigan	6	6	6	541.05
Minnesota	6	6	6	752-725, 15-1-29
Mississippi	3	3	3	516.110, 516.120
Missouri	10	10	5	27-2-202
Montana	8	8	5	25-205, 25-206
Nebraska	5	5	4	11.90
Nevada	6	6	4	508:4
New Hampshire	6	6	6	2A:14-1
New Jersey	6	6	6	37-1-3, 37-1-4
New Mexico	6	6	4	CPLR 213(2)
New York	6	6	6	CP 1-52
North Carolina	3	3	3	28-01-16
North Dakota	6	6	6	2305.06, 2305.07
Ohio	15	15	6	12 Sec. 95
Oklahoma	5	5	3	12.080
Oregon	6	6	6	42 Sec. 5525
Pennsylvania	4	4	4	9-1-13(a)
Rhode Island	10	10	10	15-3-350
South Carolina	3	3	3	15-2-13
South Dakota	6	6	6	28-3-109
Tennessee	6	6	6	16.004
Texas	4	4	2	28-12-23, 28-12-25
Utah	6	6	4	12-511
Vermont	6	6	6	8.01-246
Virginia	5	5	3	4.16.040, 4.16.080
Washington	6	6	3	55-2-6
West Virginia	10	10	5	893.43
Wisconsin	6	6	6	1-3-105
Wyoming	10	10	8	12-301
Washington, D.C.	3	3	3	

Appendix E
Frequently Referenced Laws

Consumer Credit Protection Act, USC Title 15, Chapter 41 covers disclosure requirements for most credit transactions, credit reporting agencies, and collection agencies. The Act now includes the following laws which are referenced in this book:

- Consumer Credit Cost Disclosure (Truth in Lending), Title I of 15 USC Chapter 41, and the Truth-in-Lending regulations (Regulation Z) ensuring that everyone who has a need for consumer credit is given meaningful information regarding the cost of the credit.

  Title I includes the following:

  - Fair Credit Billing Act (regulating the manner in which you are to be billed by creditors and the information which must be disclosed to you).
  - Consumer Leasing Act of 1976.
  - Credit advertising.
  [See Truth in Lending Regulations Appendices for sample calculations and disclosure form.]

- Restrictions on Garnishment are set forth in 15 USC Section 1667, Title III.

- Fair Debt Collection Practices Act, 15 USC Section 1692, Public Law 95-109 (regulating the practices of collection agencies).

- Fair Credit Reporting Act, 15 USC Section 1681, Title VI, Public Law 91-508 (regulating the practices of credit reporting agencies or credit bureaus).

11 USC U.S. Bankruptcy Code generally.
11 USC Chapter 7, Liquidation.
11 USC Chapter 13, Adjustment of Debts of an Individual with
    Regular Income (Wage Earner Plan).
29 USC Internal Revenue Code generally.
29 USC Section 6334 - Internal Revenue Exemptions.

Index

Advances (on loan), 63
Agreement for deed, 82
Annual percentage rate, 60, 61, 66
Appraisal, 79, 84
Arbitration, 105
Assets, 111, 118
Attachment, 115
Attorney, 12, 30, 32, 65, 79
Audit, 51

Balloon payments, 64, 88
Bankruptcy, 8, 15, 39, 89, 117-122, 156
Billing cycle, 72
Business debt, 16

Child support, 20, 108
Collateral, 13, 14, 96, 143
Collection agency, 25
Collectors, 26
Commercially reasonable, 96
Complaint, 143
Confession of judgment, 105
Consumer affairs offices, 149
Consumer Credit Counseling, 24
Consumer Credit Protection Act, 43, 57, 111
Consumer lease, 77-80
Consumer Leasing Act, 77, 156
Consumer reporting agencies, 37
Contingent liability, 16
Contract, 58, 102
Contract for deed, 82
Corporation, 16
County Court,
Credit report, 37, 106
Credit transactions, 58
Credit cards, 71-76

Damages, 143
Deadbeat list, 31
Deed of trust, 82, 85
Deed in lieu of foreclosure, 86
Default judgment, 103
Defendant, 102
Deferred judgment, 101, 105
Deficiency judgment, 8, 14, 83, 89, 97, 104

Deposition, 109
Disclosure, 57-70, 71, 72, 77
Divorce, 15
Due on sale clause, 85

Employment, 28, 38, 41, 113
Equity, 143
Equitable title, 143
Equity line, 62, 81, 144
Exemption, 119, 123

Fair market value, 145
Fair Credit Billing Act, 9, 73, 156
Fair Credit Leasing Act, 9
Fair Credit Reporting Act, 9, 37, 43, 156
Fair Debt Collection Practices Act, 26, 33, 156
False pretenses, 42
Federal Trade Commission, 26, 43, 153
Federal Family Support Act,
Finance charge, 60, 66
Financing statement, 98, 145
Forebearance agreement, 89
Foreclosure, 81-94, 144

Garnishments, 111, 130
Garnishment exemptions, 121, 130
Good faith estimate, 62, 68
Government Printing Office, 9, 147

Harassment, 29
Homestead, 120, 125
Housing and Urban Development (Department of), 24, 87

Insurance, 41
Internal Revenue Service, 49-55, 119
Interrogatories, 109

Joint and several liability, 17
Judgment creditor, 109
Judgment, 8, 13, 21, 24, 101
Judgment proof, 138

Land contract, 82

Leases, 17, 77
Lessee, 77
Lessor, 77, 79
Levy, 114
Lien, 144
Lost credit cards, 74

Mediation, 105
Modification of child support, 20, 108
Mortgage, 7, 13, 81, 144

Negligent, 42, 144
Noncompliance, 42
Notice of Deficiency, 50

Open-end consumer credit, 71-76

Plaintiff, 101
Problem Resolution Officer, 50, 53
Punitive damages, 144
Purchase money mortgage, 81, 145

Quit claim deed, 145

Real estate loan foreclosures, 81-94
Redemption, 84, 98
Refinancing, 64
Regulation Z, 60, 89, 90, 156
Release, 63
Repossession, 95-98, 145
Rescission, 62, 63
Residual value, 79, 145
Revised Uniform Reciprocal
   Enforcement of Support Act, 21
Right of set-off, 14
Rules of Civil Procedure, 102

Secured debt, 13, 14
Security interest, 145
Service of process, 83, 102
Set-off (See "Right of set-off")
SLMA (Student Loan Marketing As-
   sociation), 18
Small Claims Court, 102
Soldiers' and Sailors' Civil Relief Act,
88, 98
Statute of limitations, 103, 145, 154
Stolen credit cards, 74
Student loans, 18-20
Summons, 102

Tax intercepts, 18, 21
Taxes, 49-55
Taxpayers Bill of Rights, 50
Telephone orders, 59
Trustee, 118
Truth in Lending, 9, 57, 66, 156

U.S. Tax Court, 53, 55
Unconscionable, 103
Uniform Enforcement of
   Foreign Judgments Act, 104
Uniform Reciprocal Enforcement of
   Support Act, 21
Unsecured debt, 13, 15
Unsolicited credit cards, 74

Wage assignments, 24
Wage garnishments, 111
Warranty, 78, 103
Writ of execution, 114

National titles valid in all 50 States

Living Trusts & Simple Ways to Avoid Probate 19.95
Simple Ways to Protect Yourself From Lawsuits 24.95
Help Your Lawyer Win Your Case 12.95
The Most Valuable Business Forms You'll Ever Need 19.95
Debtors' Rights, A Legal Self-Help Guide, 2nd Ed. 12.95
Grandparents' Rights 19.95
Divorces From Hell 10.95
Legal Research Made Easy 14.95
The Most Valuable Corporate Forms You'll Ever Need . 24.95
How to Register Your Own Copyright 19.95
How to Register Your Own Trademark 19.95

Victims' Rights

The Complete Guide
to Crime Victim
Compensation

• Who qualifies   • How much is available
• How to qualify   • Rights of Relatives
• How to apply   • Who to contact

William L. Ginsburg
Attorney at Law

Lawsuits of the Rich & Famous 10.95
How to File Your Own Bankruptcy, 3rd Ed. 19.95
U.S.A. Immigration Guide 19.95
Guia de Inmigración a Estados Unidos 19.95
Victims' Rights 12.95
How to File Your Own Divorce 19.95
How to Write Your Own Premarital Agreement 19.95
How to Form Your Own Corporation 19.95
How to Negotiate Real Estate Contracts 14.95
How to Negotiate Real Estate Leases 14.95
Neighbor vs. Neighbor 12.95
The Power of Attorney Handbook 19.95

SELF-HELP LAW KIT

Legal Research Made Easy

With Flowcharts

Includes
State & Federal Materials
Computer Databases
Sample Research Problem

Mark Warda
Attorney at Law

SPHINX PUBLISHING

Florida Legal Guides

Landlords' Rights & Duties in Florida, 5th Ed. 19.95
How to File for Divorce in Florida, 3rd Ed. 19.95
How to Modify Your Florida Divorce Judgment, 2nd Ed. 19.95
How to Form a Simple Corporation in Florida, 3rd Ed. 19.95
How to Form a Nonprofit Corporation in Florida, 3rd Ed. 19.95
How to Win in Florida Small Claims Court, 5th Ed. 14.95
How to Probate an Estate in Florida, 2nd Ed. ...24.95
How to Start a Business in Florida, 4th Ed. 16.95
How to File a Florida Construction Lien, 2nd Ed. ..19.95
Land Trusts in Florida, 4th Ed. 24.95
How to Make a Florida Will, 3rd Ed. 9.95
How to Change Your Name in Florida, 3rd Ed. 14.95
Florida Power of Attorney Handbook 9.95
How to File for Guardianship in Florida 19.95
How to File an Adoption in Florida 19.95
Winning in Florida Traffic Court 14.95
Women's Legal Rights in Florida 19.95

SELF-HELP LAW KIT

How to File for Divorce in Florida

With Forms

Includes
Child Support
Child Custody & Visitation
Alimony

SELF-HELP LAW KIT

Landlords' Rights & Duties in Florida

With Forms
and Caselaw

Includes
Security Deposits Rules
Eviction Procedures
Residential and Commercial

Mark Warda
Attorney at Law

SPHINX PUBLISHING

Sphinx Publishing, P.O. Box 25, Clearwater, FL 34617
To Order Call: 1-800-226-5291

Southeastern Region

- Alabama
- Florida
- Georgia
- Louisiana
- Mississippi
- North Carolina
- South Carolina
- Texas

How to Register Your Own Trademark (S.E. Ed.)	$21.95
How to Form Your Own Partnership (S.E. Ed.)	$16.95

Texas

How to File for Divorce in Texas	$19.95
How to Make a Texas Will	$ 9.95
How to Start a Business in Texas	$16.95
Landlords' Rights & Duties in Texas	$19.95
How to Probate an Estate in Texas	$19.95
How to Form a Simple Corporation in Texas	$19.95
How to Win in Small Claims Court in Texas	$14.95

North Carolina

How to File for Divorce in North Carolina	$19.95
How to Make a North Carolina Will	$ 9.95
How to Start a Business in North Carolina	$16.95

Michigan

How to File for Divorce in Michigan	$19.95
How to Make a Michigan Will	$ 9.95
How to Start a Business in Michigan	$16.95

Georgia

How to File for Divorce in Georgia	$19.95
How to Make a Georgia Will	$ 9.95
How to Start and Run a Georgia Business	$ 16.95

Alabama

How to File for Divorce in Alabama	$19.95
How to Make an Alabama Will	$ 9.95
How to Start a Business in Alabama	$16.95

South Carolina

How to File for Divorce in South Carolina	$19.95
How to Make a South Carolina Will	$ 9.95
How to Start a Business in South Carolina	$16.95